The Braided Narrative: A Brief History

Other Books by Robert Alexander

Poetry

Finding Token Creek: New and Selected Writing, 1975–2020
What the Raven Said
White Pine Sucker River: Poems 1970–1990

Nonfiction

Indian Country: The Road to Fallen Timbers
A Robin's Egg Renaissance: Chicago Modernism & the Great War
The Northwest Ordinance: Constitutional Politics and the Theft of Native Land
Five Forks: Waterloo of the Confederacy — A Civil War Narrative

Anthologies .

Spring Phantoms: Short Prose by 19th Century British & American Authors
Edited by Robert Alexander
Marie Alexander Series, volume 22

Nothing to Declare: A Guide to the Flash Sequence
Edited by Robert Alexander, Eric Braun, and Debra Marquart
Marie Alexander Series, volume 20

Family Portrait: American Prose Poetry, 1900–1950
Edited by Robert Alexander
Marie Alexander Series, volume 16

The House of Your Dream: An International Collection of Prose Poetry
Edited by Robert Alexander and Dennis Maloney
Marie Alexander Series, volume 11

The Party Train: A Collection of North American Prose Poetry
Edited by Robert Alexander, Mark Vinz, and C. W. Truesdale

The Braided Narrative: A Brief History

Robert Alexander

Marie Alexander Series, Volume 25

WHITE PINE PRESS / BUFFALO, NEW YORK

White Pine Press
P.O. Box 236
Buffalo, NY 14201
www.whitepine.org

Publication of this book was supported by public funds from the New York State Council on the Arts, with the support of Governor Kathy Hochul and the New York State Legislature, a State Agency.

Acknowledgements: See page 148. The Acknowledgments page at the end of the text is an extension of this copyright page.

Cover image: *Still Life with Violin*
Georges Braque, 1913
Oil on canvas
Courtesy Los Angeles County Museum of Art

Printed and bound in the United States of America.

ISBN 978-1-945680-75-5

Library of Congress Control Number: 2024930190

*At a certain point categories break down, and that's where I
want to write: in the broken-down, wide-open spot.*
                                        —Maureen Gibbon

Contents

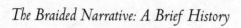

The Braided Narrative: A Brief History

I.
Introduction

It was the end of summer. I was heading back to the Midwest for my last year of college, and the feed corn was drying in the fields. My friends were all planning for the next stage of their lives—applying to law school, or med school, or just trying to figure out how to avoid having to go to Vietnam. I'd solved that last problem the previous summer while carrying my own and my girlfriend's suitcases from the Martha's Vineyard ferry: after persistent back pain, an x-ray had showed a congenital abnormality that would preclude my successfully finishing the army's basic training—but now she'd left me for an art professor and the career path I'd chosen, being a successful writer, had no manual that I could find. Grad school in English was about the last thing I wanted to do. So, as I said to myself one fall afternoon, it was time to get serious—which meant, near as I could figure, that it was time to write a novel.

I had a situation in mind, and lived with that for a while: a student who had an affair with her English teacher—a story which at that time, the late sixties, seemed to a twenty-something American male like it might have commercial potential. Then one day I heard a first sentence in my head and sat down at the typewriter—this was before computers had become a household item—and I was off and running.

> But you always said that many things were possible, not least among
> them love. And though I wasn't fool enough to believe you, I always thought
> that at least you believed yourself.
> Should I then say
> So finally you've left me. And why, just when we seemed closest, when
> it seemed that summer would at last leave us alone to pursue the bright
> course of our existence?
> I remember the spring. We held each other in the warm April darkness,
> upon the damp hillside, while the clouds rushed above us.
> You are back now, I suppose, in the Midwest, in your house on the lake.
> And do you sit there, in the heavy sweet summer darkness, while your wife
> plays you Haydn? Do you sit there thinking fondly of the art you may
> produce from some vague memory of an autumn evening and a winter's
> loneliness?

That managed to cover all the seasons in just a few sentences (misconstruing what Aristotle meant by one revolution of the sun around the earth), and used the second person, which also, at that time, seemed to me particularly inventive. Later, in a day or two, or a week, I heard another sentence—and again, off I went:

> *You walk through Customs smiling and embrace me in the same moment you remove your pack. Hi kid. You take me home to your family's apartment looking out at the city from some immense height, seagulls gliding by the living-room windows.*
>
> *The apartment is busy with a cocktail party. Feigning fatigue, you lead me to the guest room where we're served dinner by uniformed maids. After chicken cacciatore and wine you light a candle and we talk, looking out at the rainy night. We discuss your trip. You tell me, upon questioning, of your few brief affairs. Slowly we undress each other.*
>
> *In the midst of this a maid enters. We believe she stands watching us a moment before she leaves.*

This process repeated itself a dozen or perhaps two dozen times over the course of the semester—as I grew increasingly depressed—and by Christmas I had a sequence with a large number of moving parts, and an equally indeterminate coda:

> *There's a large park across the road and the water spreading blue and pristine in the afternoon. We walk across the salt-rusted bridge, the sun hot, lovers lying in the grass, dogs running in packs. The boathouse is light and sandstone, windows twenty feet high. The windows are empty now in the afternoon sunlight. The earth breathes dry, dry, dry, this summer, the cedars dark and dry.[1]*

I put a title to it—"Good Harbor" (a beach on the North Shore of Massachusetts I'd bonded with as a teenager)—with an evocative epigraph from Ernest Dowson:

> . . . one by one
> The roses fall, the pale roses expire
> Beneath the slow decadence of the sun.

But this was a long way from what I'd had in mind when I first sat down to write a novel—which was of course the cause of my depression, as I saw my fantasy of a brilliant career disappearing into wisps of marijuana smoke. As I wrote later,

> It was the year that Rod Stewart sang about Maggie May and there I was going back to school with the feed corn drying in September. I was going to be a world-class novelist and this was the year it would happen, me holed up in a farmhouse outside of town with wood heat and a small writing desk beneath the window that overlooked alfalfa fields and the oak-scattered hills. . . .
>
> It didn't happen that way. I never saw her again and the novel I wrote ended up serving for the most part to ignite the wood in the stove.[2]

As I decided one afternoon in a fit of self-shaming, I'd been writing "some sort of shrunken, deformed story that I was too lazy to transform into a piece of *real* fiction":

> This was long before the term *flash* had been applied to fiction in any but a marketing sense, and *short-shorts* still referred to an item of clothing. For a while I told anyone who would listen that I was writing, or attempting to write, "experimental fiction." While it was true that these pieces, strung together as a sequence, did hint at an underlying theme, a montage-like connection of some sort between the disparate sections, in a traditional sense they lacked pretty much all semblance of a plot.[3]

There were, of course, plenty of other people who'd done this same sort of thing, most of them more successfully—though at the time I was unaware of most of it. The most recent example I'd read was Robert Coover's *Pricksongs & Descants*—and I was delighted when I discovered it—and around that same time I also found Diane di Prima's *Dinners & Nightmares*. But what was I to do with my "experiments"? After all, my intention had been to write a *novel*. In the half-century since then, there have been a number of such things published—going by the name of "a novel in pieces," or some such characterization—but this was many years ago, and my feeble attempts didn't bode well for my dream of making a living as a writer.

After many long months I began to admit defeat. I decided to focus on the fragments themselves, rather than on the sequence-of-fragments. I realized that such disconnected pieces of short prose were beginning to garner a certain attention in the Anglophone literary world as the so-called prose poem. If I played my cards right, I thought, I might be able to make a career out of studying this peculiar literary creature's history, theory, and practice. I thought, if I worked hard enough at it, I might be able to turn out little jewel boxes that would fascinate my readers. So as I've said elsewhere, I made it my mission "to justify the ways of the prose poem to poets and critics alike."

As the *poème en prose*, its history in French literature was well-known, but the fact that the form also had a long history in Anglo-American literature was, at that time, little understood. Indeed, it carried with it a certain disrepute in English letters: one critic, for example, calling it "a genre whose spiritual inconveniences it takes very tough creative discipline to stand up under."[4]

Over the course of my career in prose poetry, such as it's been, I came across many attempts at narrative sequences. Though the various incarnations of the vignette itself became my focus, each collection of my own poetry or anthology of others' writing I helped to compile contained a few sequences. In fact, all the examples in this book have been drawn from them. In 2016, Eric Braun and Debra Marquart and I edited a collection of work we called "flash sequences," and our original intention was to include some important historical examples. But space limitations precluded that option.

In a call for manuscripts we made the following assertion: "For several decades writers and publishers have focused on prose shorts, calling them by various names: prose poems, short shorts, flash fiction, lyric essays, and so forth. Yet no one has seriously considered the nature of sequences of such forms." We gave prospective authors as little direction as possible, our intention being to let them decide, with just a few guidelines, what to submit: an accumulation (as we called it) of two or more prose pieces, with each segment not to exceed 500 words, and a total submission not to exceed 10 pages. "We encourage submissions of every sort; rather than try to define the form, we hope each writer will use whatever organizing principle seems best in any particular case: fiction, nonfiction, prose-poetry, or whatever."

✻ ✻ ✻

One of the most important sequences which I include here, in its entirety, is Ernest Hemingway's "In Our Time"—finally, after ninety-five years, it having emerged from copyright protection. A truncated excerpt from this series of short sketches first appeared in the fall 1923 issue of the *Little Review*—"Exile's Number" (edited by Ezra Pound)—which was, for financial reasons, not published until early in 1924. An expanded version—titled *in our time*—was published in Paris the same year as a chapbook by Bill Bird's Three Mountains Press, and its sections (titled "chapters") were later incorporated between the short stories of Hemingway's first commercial collection, also titled *In Our Time* (Boni & Liveright, 1925). The Three Mountains version is the one presented here.[5]

Hemingway's chapbook is an excellent example of a genre (if you can call it that), which, as I discovered, has been common since the twenties at least. It has little narrative thread; the eighteen separate scenes are related at the level of abstraction (war, violence, birth, violent death), but there's no clear fictional structure, though each piece is clearly narrative in tone, using techniques of direct observation, of simplicity of diction and syntax, that elsewhere I've talked about in relation to American prose poems.

Edmund Wilson, reviewing *In Our Time* for the *Dial* in 1924, says that Hemingway's writing—"a distinctively American development in prose"— is characterized by "a naivete of language . . . which serves actually to convey profound emotions and complex states of mind." By using "dry compressed little vignettes," Wilson says that Hemingway "has almost invented a form of his own." And he concludes that this "harrowing record of barbarities . . . has more artistic dignity than any other that has been written by an American about the period of the war."[6]

This sort of experimentation was common among modernist writers. In *transition workshop*, for example—drawn from the pages of *transition* magazine—Eugene Jolas included prose sequences by James Joyce, Dylan Thomas, Jolas himself, and Harry Crosby, among others.[7] William Carlos Williams' *Kora in Hell: Improvisations*, published in 1920, is a series of twenty-seven prose sequences, some of which appeared first in the *Little Review*, with each sequence composed of three sections, plus in some cases an italicized "note." As Williams says regarding their organization,

> I have placed the following Improvisations in groups, some-
> what after the ABA formula, that one may support the other,
> clarifying or enforcing perhaps the other's intentions. The ar-
> rangement of the notes, each following its poem and sep-
> arated from it by a ruled line, is borrowed from a small
> volume of Metastasio, *Varie Poesie Dell'Abate Pietro Metastasio*,
> Venice, 1795.[8]

As Williams seems to be telling us here, it shouldn't be imagined that the prose sequence is a twentieth century invention. William Blake's *Marriage of Heaven and Hell* (published in 1790) fits the description, as does Walt Whitman's *Memoranda during the War*, which was later incorporated into *Specimen Days* (1883).

* * *

If one purpose of literary art is to pass along the stories of the tribe to the next generation, we can agree that an important model for literature—the so-called oral-formulaic tradition—involves the bardic elder entertaining his or her audience around a campfire. This forms the basis of what we call *narrative*. But there's another model as well—beginning in ritual, in dance and music—which develops characters who quite literally *embody* the action directly. We call this *drama*, and Aristotle, in his *Poetics*, gives us the two authorial examples of Homer and Sophocles. Sequence, indeed, lies at the very root of both forms.

We can tell the same basic story in either way—drama or narrative—as Susan Glaspell has done with her play, "Trifles" (1916), and her story, "A Jury of Her Peers" (1917), both loosely based upon a murder case she reported for the Des Moines *Daily News*. When playwrights or novelists divide their action, they are constructing a sequence. Over the long course of human cultural history, this endeavor has grown into all the varied novels, Broadway shows, television series—and, not least, the multi-million-dollar movies that have come to define the so-called entertainment industry. In fact, my own conception of sequence, or of montage, in part traces its lineage to cinema.

In 1929, Sergei Eisenstein laid out a precise definition of montage. He starts with a quote from Goethe: "In nature we never see anything isolated, but everything in connection with something else which is before it, beside it, under it, and over it." He goes on to say that "shot and montage are the basic elements of cinema . . . [and] to determine the nature of montage is to solve the specific problem of cinema." Rather than being limited to the sort of sequential chronological narrative found in stage drama, "montage is an idea that arises from the collision of independent shots—shots even opposite to one another." Eisenstein turns then to language itself: "a concrete word (a denotation) set beside a concrete word yields an abstract concept—as in the Chinese and Japanese languages, where a material ideogram can indicate a transcendental (conceptual) result."

So cinematic sequences can follow a non-narrative structure. As Eisenstein asks, "Now why should the cinema follow the forms of theater and painting rather than the methodology of language, which allows wholly new concepts of ideas to arise from the combination of two concrete denotations of two concrete objects?" Each piece in a sequence "can evoke no more than a certain association"—and "the accumulation of such associations . . . will be an all-embracing complex of emotional feeling." Eisenstein concludes that this process "can be formally identified with that of logical deduction," or "a kind of filmic reasoning."[9]

In other words, each sequence contains its own sort of progression, which affects the reader, in the end, as a unified work of art. The possibilities inherent in this notion of sequence are pretty much limitless.

—Robert Alexander

II.
A Simple Sequence Is a Pair

Sitting in the Dunes Saloon in Grand Marais, Michigan, one summer afternoon, Jim Harrison told me that he had finally figured out how to write a prose poem: "Just go straight from beginning to end, and forget the middle," he said, sipping his vodka. This was, I gathered, for someone who had perfected the art of circumlocution—like another master story-teller, Ford Madox Ford—no simple matter.

If A, then B. By this way of thinking, every sonnet constitutes a sequence. But who can ask of a sonnet that each section be complete by it-self—that the octave must stand on its own as a poem, and the sestet as well? Instead, we ask only that the entire poem be what we might call self-reli-ant—and so we ask of a sequence only that it be of a piece, entire. Which is to say: for the prose sequence to be successful, it must itself function as a unity—that is, as a piece of art surrounded by the frame of silence.

Some sequences are indeed composed of integral sections, with their own titles, complete within themselves. In every case the ultimate judge of that must be the reader. Moreover, there's another aspect of the prose sequence which only the reader can address. Elsewhere I've attempted to an-swer the question, How does a (prose) poem differ from (flash) fiction? The sequence, like the individual pieces which compose it, can partake of the quality of both fiction (or nonfiction) and of poetry—of narrative or of lyric—and it's only the individual reader who determines which quality, in any particular case, predominates.[10]

Whatever the particular example, whether it strikes one overall more as narrative or as lyric, what we can say for sure is that every sequence is more than the sum of its parts. The multitude of ways in which interrelated sections can fit together is precisely why the prose sequence is so fascinating: from a nearly-seamless narrative to a fragmented, hallucinatory reverie. The simplest sequence is a pair, beginning and end.

Jane Heap (1883–1964)[11]

WHITE

I

Sharp, empty air. . . . Out of the black mouths of engines white smoke rises on thin stems into white ghosts of ancient trees; together they rise into ghosts of ancient forests, sway and surge and are gone again a million years.

II

The hot air of the day stays in the city until night. The long slope of my roof presses the heat down upon me. Soon it will rain. But there is no rest in me: my heart is wandering too far. My friends may still be in the city, but I do not seek them. I go to the animals in the park. Within their enclosures black shadows of camels lie in the darkness. A great white camel broods in the moonlight, apart from the rest. His lonely eyes are closed and he moves his head slowly from side to side on his long neck, swaying in pain, searching in a dream for his lost world. I have seen a Norwegian ship carrying its carved head through the waters of a fjord with such a movement. . . .

Now the high clouds cover the moon. Out on the lake a wind assails the layers of heat. A white peacock sits in a tree, aloof, elegant, incorruptible. . . . A light green spirit. . . . Across the first thunder he lifts his long white laugh at us like a maniac.

T. S. Eliot (1888–1965)[12]

THE ENGINE

I

The engine hammered and hummed. Flat faces of American businessmen lay along the tiers of chairs in one plane, broken only by the salient of a brown cigar and the red angle of a six-penny magazine. The machine was hard, deliberate, and alert; having chosen with motives and ends unknown to cut through the fog it pursued its course; the life of the deck stirred and was silent like a restless scale on the smooth surface. The machine was certain and sufficient as a rose bush, indifferently justifying the aimless parasite.

II

After the engine stopped, I lay in bed listening while the wash subsided and the scuffle of feet died out. The music ceased, but a mouth organ from the steerage picked up the tune. I switched on the light, only to see on the wall a spider taut as a drumhead, the life of endless geological periods concentrated into a small spot of intense apathy at my feet. "And if the ship goes down" I thought drowsily "he is prepared and will somehow persist, for he is very old. But the flat faces. . . ." I tried to assemble these nebulae into one pattern. Failing, I roused myself to hear the machine recommence, and then the music, and the feet upon the deck.

Thornton Wilder (1897–1975)[13]

SENTENCES

I

In the Italian quarter of London I found a group of clerks, waiters and idealistic barbers calling itself The Rosicrucian Mysteries, Soho Chapter, that met to read papers on the fabrication of gold and its metaphysical implications, to elect from its number certain Arch-adepts and *magistri hieraticorum*, to correspond with the last of the magi, Orzinda-mazda, on Mt. Sinai, and to retell, wide-eyed, their stories of how some workmen near Rome, breaking by chance into the tomb of Cicero's daughter, Tulliola, discovered an ever-burning lamp suspended in mid-air, its wick feeding on Perpetual Principle; of how Cleopatra's son Caesarion was preserved in a translucent liquid, "oil of gold," and could be still seen in an underground shrine at Vienna; and of how Virgil never died, but was alive still on the Island of Patmos, eating the leaves of a peculiar tree.

II

In Rome I encountered a number of people who for one reason or another were unable to sleep between midnight and dawn, and when I tossed sleepless, or when I returned late to my rooms through the deserted streets—at the hour when the parricide feels a cat purring about his feet in the darkness—I pictured to myself old Baldassare in the Borgo, former Bishop of Shantung and Apostolic Visitor to the Far East, rising at two to study with streaming eyes the Fathers and the Councils, marveling, he said, at the continuous blooming of the rose-tree of Doctrine; or of Stasia, a Russian refugee who had lost the habit of sleeping after dark during her experience as nurse in the War, Stasia playing solitaire through the night and brooding over the jocose tortures to which her family had been subjected by the soldiers of Taganrog; and of Elizabeth Grier who, like some German prince of the Eighteenth Century, owned her own band of musicians, listening the length over her long shadowed room to some new work that D'Indy had sent her, or bending over the score while her little troupe revived the overture to *Les Indes Galantes*.

Robert Bly (1926–2021)[14]

THE DEAD SEAL

I.

Walking north toward the point, I come on a dead seal. From a few feet away, he looks like a brown log. The body is on its back, dead only a few hours. I stand and look at him. There's a quiver in the dead flesh: My God, he's still alive. And a shock goes through me, as if a wall of my room had fallen away.

His head is arched back, the small eyes closed; the whiskers sometimes rise and fall. He is dying. This is the oil. Here on its back is the oil that heats our houses so efficiently. Wind blows fine sand back toward the ocean. The flipper near me lies folded over the stomach, looking like an unfinished arm, lightly glazed with sand at the edges. The other flipper lies half underneath. And the seal's skin looks like an old overcoat, scratched here and there—by sharp mussel shells maybe.

I reach out and touch him. Suddenly he rears up, turns over. He gives three cries: Awaark! Awaark! Awaark!—like the cries from Christmas toys. He lunges toward me; I am terrified and leap back, though I know there can be no teeth in that jaw. He starts flopping toward the sea. But he falls over, on his face. He does not want to go back to the sea. He looks up at the sky, and he looks like an old lady who has lost her hair. He puts his chin back down on the sand, rearranges his flippers, and waits for me to go. I go.

2.

The next day I go back to say good-bye. He's dead now. But he's not. He's a quarter mile farther up the shore. Today he is thinner, squatting on his stomach, head out. The ribs show much more: each vertebra on the back under the coat is visible, shiny. He breathes in and out.

A wave comes in, touches his nose. He turns and looks at me—the eyes slanted; the crown of his head looks like a boy's leather jacket bending over some bicycle bars. He is taking a long time to die. The whiskers white as porcupine quills, the forehead slopes . . . . Goodbye, brother, die in the sound of the waves. Forgive us if we have killed you. Long live your race, your inner-tube race, so uncomfortable on land, so comfortable in the ocean. Be comfortable in death then, when the sand will be out of your nostrils, and you can swim in long loops through the pure death, ducking under as assassinations break above you. You don't want to be touched by me. I climb the cliff and go home the other way.

Michael Benedikt (1935–2007)[15]

HOW TO DISEMBARK FROM A LARK

(1) The little ladder has been placed in position and everybody is climbing up the staircase onto its back. And, look, already its wings are beginning to beat in anticipation! Little clouds of dust are coming out from both sides now. Now, everybody is seated in neat rows on its back and set for flight. This is precisely when you begin to experience, for some unknown reason, a certain feeling of uneasiness. So you begin to wonder: is this lark you are on truly prudent? No: logic has not deserted you yet! At once, displaying your customary perspicacity, you start to disembark. You grab your hat, you grab your coat, you grab your luggage and lorgnette, and begin to call out for the porter to throw your suitcases out from beneath the pinfeathers. But suddenly you sense waves of disapproval beginning to radiate your way. "Oh, what a spoil-sport," somebody cries out from beneath the beak, "in such a hurry to depart, and the trip only just begun!" Wimbles are coming from the smoking-lounge! The words "party pooper" a rumor in the Piano Bar! But still, your customary control and logic continue to dominate. For, as the lark begins to run across the field, you realize, with perfect lucidity, that if you're ever going to leave this lark, this could be your last chance right now! Abandoning your luggage, abandoning the little ladder, abandoning everything but your understanding, you fling yourself off into space, into the very teeth of the breeze, just beneath the snap of its beak, and the whizz of its retracting legs. For fully five minutes after touchdown you tumble around on the runway in the wake of its windy slipstream.

(2) No, you think. In your most lucid moments of all, you wonder whether once a person is committed to such a venture, it is ever in fact truly prudent to disembark from a lark.

Julie Stotz-Ghosh (1970–   )[16]

HAIKU SEQUENCE FOR SNOW

I.

Frances counts syllables in the first poem of her new series: "Haiku Sequence for Snow." *All afternoon, low gray clouds.* Seven. Living in Michigan, you know snow is coming when the clouds get low and gray, light gray, like cement (not the angry, dark gray of thunder clouds, the kind that seem to roll in, the kind that tower and intimidate). Snow clouds cover the sky like a blanket, but she can't write "cover the sky like a blanket." She can't write that snow clouds and short December days make her sad; she has to show it. *Wind chases snow down the street.* Seven. She is snow; wind is sadness. *Wind makes sport of snow.* Five. She doesn't think you'll understand.

She's tired of games. She wants to write: *I'm lonely in my house because even the furnace sounds like wind whipping snow off the roof,* but she can't write, "like wind whipping snow." She wants to write: *Icicles look sinister like pointed animal teeth along the gutters of my neighbors' houses,* but she can't write, "like pointed animal teeth." She wants to write: *My brother is unfairly mad at me because I forgot to pay him for the honey he gave me straight from the hives of his bees, the honey he had to boil especially for me so that I could give it as holiday presents to my neighbors who live inside ice-covered homes,* but she can't write, "hives of his bees," or "holiday presents," or "ice-covered homes," and don't even bother counting the syllables.

She feels ice-covered. She wants you to know that it's a metaphor for loss. She's afraid you won't understand. She wants to write, *I lost a baby.* Five. But she can't write "baby" or "lost."

2.

When she was young enough to curl into small spaces, Frances liked to fall asleep like a cat against her mother in the blue light of late-night news shows. In the blue light of the ultrasound room, Frances watches images that look like snow-covered mountains—outer space satellite transmissions of white river beds. The technician maps out hills and valleys, measures distances. Everything is winter. Outside, December breaks its promise. Snow melts—drips and slides off buildings and cars. Icicles fall wickedly in chunks from eaves.

When it's time to leave, Frances can't remember where she parked her car. People walk in circles around her, talking loudly.

III.
How Sophocles Invented Fiction

In my estimation, it can be said that Sophocles invented fiction. According to Aristotle, "Aeschylus first introduced a second actor; he diminished the importance of the Chorus, and assigned the leading part to the dialogue." But it was Sophocles who "raised the number of actors to three, and added scene-painting."[17]

In physics, there is something known as the three-body problem. While it is easy, given the ubiquity of gravitation, to predict the exact positions of two objects, going forward, if one knows initial conditions—position, mass, velocity—it is impossible to do so, in a single equation, for a system containing three or more objects. The problem is too complex for our mathematics, and the only solutions possible are chaotic—that is, a small change in initial conditions can cause wildly different outcomes. Likewise, a narrative that introduces more than two characters sets the stage for an unpredictable chain of events, and it's because of the resulting suspense that we stay awake nights reading to find out the conclusion of the novel.

Sometimes, indeed, there are only two characters, the lover and his or her beloved, but in lieu of other characters there's an offscreen presence that provides a third entity: the evil step-parent or the distant war or the Church. In Jack London's "To Build a Fire," for example, the weather itself is a character, along with Man and Dog—asserting its dominance when a pine overhead buries the man's fire in a mound of smoking snow.

This quality of interpersonal tension is what I associate, in its essence, with fiction. Plot in a story, novel, or film involves the working-through of this multi-body problem, the resolution of this tension over time. There are works of poetry that contain this same tension, but we conceive of them as poems rather than fiction. Take, for example, Shakespeare's sonnets, with the Poet, his Beloved, and the mysterious Other Man. If written in prose, the sonnets would compose a narrative sequence—each individual piece capturing a single emotional configuration—but as they're written in verse we focus less on the implied or hidden "plot" and more on the writing itself, each piece shining with what Walter Pater, in another context, called a hard, gem-like flame.

The sequence in three parts is, perhaps, the model for all literature: beginning, middle, and end. Though Jim Harrison's simplest of prose poems has only an end and a beginning, in a three-part sequence there's always a middle, though it might be a single sentence, a paragraph, or several. Furthermore, a braid—as any long-haired kid can tell you—must consist of at least three separate strands—which is to say, there's no way to weave two strands together in the same way as three or more: "I remember watching with fascination as my sister and her friends plaited their hair on long weekend afternoons in the country, the rain streaming down along the living-room windows that faced out across the cornfields."

Another model for a three-part narrative might be a logical (or illogical) syllogism: all cats are gray at night; now it's nighttime; therefore I have a gray cat. But of course there are other possibilities as well.

Harrison G. Rhodes (1871–1929)[18]

SKETCHES

I have been copying an essay steadily all the evening. My head aches, my fingers are wearied, and as I stare with blinking eyes at the glaring white paper, the letters I have scrawled on it dance in the brilliant lamp-light like demons. I close my eyes and I put my hand to my head in utter exhaustion. After a minute I open my eyes and say to myself,

"I will finish this page and then stop."

I go on.

. . . The prologue began with these peculiarly Johnsonian lines,

"Pressed by the load of life the weary mind
Surveys the general toil of humankind." . . .

It is too much. I throw down my pen with fierce despair. It lands on the point and stands erect on the blotting paper which covers the desk. I get up. The rain is pouring monotonously down; my fire is flickering out; I can hear my chum snoring in his bed; the clock strikes two.

"General toil of humankind. Nonsense! As if any fool but myself were working at this time."

I go to the window. Across the street, in a glare of light in one of the windows, I see two Chinamen ironing shirts.

*   *   *

In the days when Brigham Young was directing the theocratic government of Utah, the Mormon missionaries in England converted a one-legged man near Dulwich. This man, now strong in faith, conceived the idea that the prophet in Salt Lake City might effect a miraculous restoration of the leg which he had lost in an accident. So a month later he presented himself, weary and travel-stained, but full of cheerful hope, before the head of the Mormon church, and told his desires. Strange as it may seem, the prophet said he would willingly get him a new leg; but begged him first to consider the matter fully. This life, he told him, is but a vale of tears and as nothing compared to eternity. He was making the choice of going through life with one leg and having two after the resurrection, or of having two legs through

37

life and three after. The man found the prospect of being a human tripod through all eternity so uncongenial that he accepted with resignation his present lot and excused the prophet from performing the miracle.

* * *

The chancel screen is twined with evergreen and bound with holly. Through its dark bars, the white reredos gleams with its candles, brighter than ever, as if seen in the blaze of sunlight through twining vines and undergrowth from out the darkness of the woods. Against the whiteness on the altar table shines the vivid scarlet of the flowers in the vases. Before the altar kneel the acolytes in their red gowns: on either side, the choir boys in black and white. Above their heads hang the brass lamps with their little crimson flames: the middle one, hanging lowest, sways gently to and fro, as if keeping time to the monotonous intonations of the priest's chant. I watch its swinging, and as thoughts wander I follow its little light till I blink and my eyes fill with tears. Then I look away to the carved heads on the pillars above the organ and down again to the white-haired organist. As I watch him, the organ sends out a soft thread of melody which ripples down from the faint high notes of the treble—like the music of the descent of the Holy Grail in "Lohengrin." I slip mechanically back into my seat: the prayer is ended.

H. D. (1886–1961)[19]

PROSE CHORUS

Strophe.

. . . I love you would have no application for the moment. I love you waits with cold wings furled; stands a cold angel shut up like cherry-buds; cherry-buds not yet half in blossom. The cold rain and the mist and the scent of wet grass is in the unpronounceable words, I love you.

. . . I love you would have no possible application. It would tear down the walls of the city and abstract right and grace from the frozen image that might have right and grace pained upon its collar bones. The Image has no right decoration for the moment, is swathed in foreign and barbaric garment, is smothered out in the odd garments of its strange and outlandish disproportion.

. . . the Nordic image that stands and is cold and has that high mark of queen-grace upon its Nordic forehead is dying . . . is dying . . . it is dying, its buds are infolded. If once the light of the sheer beauty of the Initiate could strike its feature, it would glow like rare Syrian gold; the workmanship of the East would have to be astonishingly summoned to invent new pattern of palm branch, new decoration of pine-bud and the cone of the Nordic pine that the Eastern workman would so appropriately display twined with the Idaian myrtle. The Idaian myrtle would be shot with the enamel of the myrtle-blue that alone among workmen, the Idaian workmen fashioned in glass and in porphyry, stained to fit separate occasion and the right and perfect slicing of the rose-quartz from the Egyptian quarry.

. . . the Nordic Image is my Image and alone of all Images I would make it suitable so that the South should not laugh, so that the West should be stricken, so that the East should fall down, bearing its scented baskets of spice-pink and little roses.

Antistrophe.

. . . flowers fall, unreasonable, out of space and counter point of time beaten by the metronome of year and year, century on century. The metronome is wound up, will go on, go on beating for our life span; a metronome tick of year, year, year; life for life; heartbeat on heartbeat, beats the metronome holding us to the music that is the solid rhythm of the scale of the one, two, three, four; one, two, three, four, I am here, you are there; tell me I am here and I will tell you, you are there; but the metronome ticks a metronome music and the voice flinging its challenge to all music in the teeth of Reason stays for no tick, tick; the heart that springs to the feet of Love with all unreason, stays no moment to listen to the human tick and tick of the human metronome heart-beat.

. . . heart you are beating, heart you are beating, I am afraid to measure my heart beat by your heart beat for I am afraid with the shame of a child struck across fingers by the master that says play soft, play loud, play one-two-three-four again, again. I am struck across the fingers and across the mouth. My mouth aches with the unutterable insult of one-two-three-four.

. . . O, friend or enemy. Why can't I cry out, fall at your feet or you at my feet, one or the other overcome by the beauty of the metronome whose beauty is unassailable, or overwhelmed, overcome by the fragrance, dripped, ripped, sputtered, spread or spilt!

Epode.

. . . voiceless, without a voice, seeking areas of consciousness without you. Seeking with you areas of consciousness that without you would no . more be plausible. Set up choros against acted drama, the high boot, the gilt wreath of ivy for some dramatic deity; set him forth, crown him with paste-board pomegranates . . . pasteboard pomegranates have nothing to do with this reality. Out of the air, into the air, the color flames and there is pulse of thyme, fire-blue that leads me across a slab of white-hot marble. My feet burn there and the wet garment clings so that I am a nymph risen from white water. So you over-seeing, burn into my flesh until my bones are burnt through and attacking the marrow of my singular bone-structure, you light the flame that makes me cry toward Delphi. Were pasteboard pomegranates of any worth or plums stitched on to a paper crown? Listen . . . men re-counted your valor, shut you up in strophes, collected you in pages whose singular letters are still laced across your spirit. The Greek letters are an arabesque shutting you in, away, away; you are shut in from the eyes that read Greek letters. Take away the gold and manifest chryselephantine of your manifest decoration and you are left . . . seeping into wine-vats, creeping under closed doors, lying beside me . . .

Kay Boyle (1902–1992)[20]

JANUARY 24, NEW YORK

I

In one corner of the dormitory, near the roof, was a pigeon-cote in which more than fifty birds were cooing. The chief prisoner was a pigeon-fancier, the warden said with an apologetic smile. The detectives shifted their cigars in their mouths and looked wearily around the room. "Why, he's so soft-hearted he has to leave the building when the cook's killing one of the birds for his supper," the warden went on. "You know what he's in for?" snapped the commissioner. "Burglary, felonious assault, and homicide."

II

The detectives went through the first tier of cells in the west wing, throwing out everything they found. The prisoners were driven out and they huddled at the end of the flats, some of them rouged, their eyebrows painted, two holding blankets around their naked shoulders. Out from the cells sailed corsets, compacts, perfume bottles, a blonde wig, nightgowns, high-heeled slippers and ladies' underwear. The detectives went up to the second tier and herded the prisoners out. "I wouldn't work here for a thousand berries a week," a detective said. "I'm just not that kind of a girl."

III

The commissioner remarked that such characteristics were common in prison, but that it was disgusting to see them flaunted in this way. He didn't think he'd ever get over the shame of what he'd seen. The kingpin had a great weakness for lemonade, said the warden with an indulgent smile. The detectives pried open the locker in his cell: it was filled with tinned peaches, olives, pickled herrings, malted milk, copies of *The New Yorker*, and a deck of heroin. "If you lay a finger on my rosary," said the kingpin in a high falsetto, "I warn you I'll scream."

Nina Nyhart (1934–   )[21]

GHOST TRIPTYCH

My mother's not dead yet, only wandering, not knowing if she's in one place or another. So she comes to sit beside me easily, more easily than in the past. And she disappears easily, as she often did. As I drive along, my mother's ghost flinches, shrinks from the savage traffic. What can you expect, I say, we're in Boston. Stoplight. She squirms impatiently. I remind her how lucky we are to be together, here, after so many years apart. She grows silent, and finally, as if love were the result of an algebraic equation she must work out, she agrees.

*   *   *

My father's ghost often visits my mother. He spends afternoons with her talking over the old days. He finds her no matter where she has wandered to—Philadelphia, the Gulf Coast—and today, on shipboard. Don't worry, she tells me over the phone, the ship is tied securely to the dock, and someone is cooking dinner. She's growing cold, though, the ship's in Alaska now—serious fishing—and so many men washed overboard. Such a harsh life, fishing.

*   *   *

I go to starlight as to a beautiful woman, my mother, wearing a long white silk jersey dress of the thirties, Hollywood style. She sits at the skirted dressing table before the triptych mirror combing her dark wavy hair. Three women open their lipsticks, apply crimson to their lips, dab Nuit de Noel on their throats. She puts on her diamond pin and earrings all shaped like stars. They sparkle in the dark room—starlight—and when I reach to touch it, it's gone, back into that darkness she shone from for a few minutes, long ago.

Pamela Painter (1941–)[22]

ART TELLS US . . .

I. *What I See*

Those sinewy lines are real. I'm standing on the edge of a friend's blue tile swimming pool, and just this instant I realize that those lines I saw and was amused by in a David Hockney painting are the real thing. I turn to call to my wife but she is deep in conversation with Max, who is generously mixing her one of his slushy margaritas. His wife is sunbathing, against all reason, her eyes closed. I turn back to those yellow wavy lines in my friend's pool. I'm seeing them for the first time. Hockney has made me see something I discounted in his painting as an artist's license to paint anything. Even silly lines. These lines must be ridges reflecting the Cape summer sun—lines most apparent in Hockney's painting *Peter Getting out of Nick's Pool*. Sinewy lines made up of thin reeds of red and orange, and before this moment totally unbelievable.

At the MFA exhibit, I marveled at the nerve of Hockney to paint those lines, when his rendering of Peter's naked back as he perhaps contemplates getting out of the pool is so marvelously real. His hands flat on the hot concrete surrounding the pool. His wide shoulders hunched around his neck, his head turned to the right, his mouth hidden by his raised right shoulder. Strong shoulders taper to a waist, then the slight flare of hips made for holding on to when what I thought of as imaginary lines approach his bare buttocks. His cleft is a rich sienna or raw umber slash with one wavery, solid watery line in particular moving through his slightly parted legs—a line that surely ends somewhere. Peter is looking off to the right—he doesn't seem to be getting out of the pool. Perhaps he is looking for Nick. Perhaps he is waiting for an invitation. Perhaps the tension in his arms is the real invitation.

Hockney has made me see. I look around my friend's pool to see what else I see. I see hummingbirds with invisible wings, crimson trumpet vines eclipsing whatever structure lies beneath its canopy, becoming the more solid of the two. I see my wife deep in conversation with my best friend, Max—her gaze locked on his, their drinks held in silent salutation, an in-

43

visible filament between them as tangible, as breakable now, as glass.

II. *A View*: Office at Night

They don't seem to be working, though up to a few minutes ago she was filing papers in a tall filing cabinet. Beside the cabinet, her boss sits reading a page at his desk, holding it beneath a green banker's light. Her plump right arm bends to encompass a generous bosom, and her right hand rests on the edge of the open drawer. Seconds ago she turned toward the man at the desk. Her face is vulnerable, intent. She is waiting. Partly hidden by the desk, a piece of paper lies on the floor between her and the man at the desk. We are led to believe that Edward Hopper is in a train, passing by on the El. The most voluptuous curve in all of Hopper's paintings, almost to a surreal degree, belongs to this secretary in the night-blue dress in *Office at Night*, an oil on canvas, 1940. What word, in 1940, would have been used to describe those two rounded globes beneath the stretch of the blue dress's skirt?

If it weren't for that piece of paper on the floor, we might believe the curator's prim description of this painting: "The secretary's exaggerated sexualized persona contrasts with the buttoned-up indifference of her boss; the frisson of their intimate overtime is undermined by a sense that the scene's erotic expectations are not likely to be met."

Wrong! The man is not indifferent. He is intent on the paper he is reading—but too intent, and he is not sitting head-on at his desk. He is turned—slightly—toward the secretary, his left elbow firmly on the desk, and his right elbow nearer her is uncomfortably balanced on the desk's edge. His mouth is slightly open as if to speak. His left ear is red. It is. It is red.

And what of their day. Her desk faces his in this small cramped office. They have no privacy because the wall to the hallway beyond does not reach the ceiling. He must have looked up from his papers, glanced up from his desk to say to her as she faced him behind her black typewriter, that tonight they must stay late. Did the secretary call her mother, or the two roommates she met while attending Katherine Gibbs, to say her boss asked her to stay late? By this time, on other evenings, she would have finished dinner, perhaps been mending her stockings, or watching the newsreel preceding the cinema's double feature.

Tonight she is working late. Yes, her dress has a chaste white collar, but the deep V of the neckline will surely fall open when she stoops to retrieve the paper that was dropped. She is looking at the paper. Was it she who dropped it? Though another object lies solidly on the chair behind her? Or did her boss drop the paper—and she is acknowledging this before she follows through on stooping over, perhaps bending at the knees over her spiffy black pumps, to retrieve the page. It resembles the papers on his desk. But note that another paper, curved slightly, its edge rising, has been nudged toward the desk's edge. The topmost paper shows a refusal to lie flat in the slight breeze from the window. This evening breeze is blowing the blind into the office, has curved the pull-cord with its sweet, soft ring. Other papers, but not all, are held in place by the 1940's black telephone, so heavy that in a B movie it could do service as the murder weapon.

Perhaps this story began at an earlier time. It might already be a situation, a situation that just this morning made the young woman choose to wear this particular blue dress. A dress equal to a request to stay late in the office at night. Somehow we are all in the middle of their drama. It isn't over yet. We are mesmerized by the piece of paper on the floor. She will bend before him. Someone will turn off the lights. Certainly they will leave before midnight. Perhaps it won't turn out well; maybe nothing good can come of this. But for now the blue dress cannot be ignored. Hopper's brush painting her, painting her dress blue, made sure of that.

III. *Artist as Guest in the Hamptons*

First of all, his wife informed him, we can't possibly have the Horstels to dinner with the Jimm Smythhs because the long dining room wall—the only space large enough for the 6' by 15' paintings they each gave us—is occupied, so to speak. Hanging there is that sixty-pound oil and gouache titled *Whale and Water* that Xu Xui announced was her "house-gift" in the thank you note she sent express mail a month after her three-week stay. Remember, since she used real glass, 'Whale and Water' was too heavy when we tried to lug it down to the basement.

He remembered all too well. Besides, he was still feeling the after-effects of last fall's hernia from carrying the Lindstrom bronze porpoise from the potting shed to the patio when Sven Lindsrom mentioned he was coming to visit them in the Hamptons to reinvigorate his artistic vision. And no doubt acquire another muse, his wife said. So in addition to having the Horstels and Smythhs separately to dinner we'll have to wait till our roaming son Charlie is home from his RISDI internship to unseat the Xu Xui and haul either the Horstel or Smythh up from the basement, depending on the guest list, to the "place of honor" in the dining room. There the artist was always circumspectly seated across from his or her work, which occasionally had a stultifying effect on conversation, but could also lead to some interesting anecdotes, like the story Tioni used to tell about his painted wooden leg's adventures in Italy before he died. Lord knows where in the garage Tioni's *Afternoon of the Fun* is buried.

Meanwhile, his wife said, about tomorrow's dinner party: the small, lush Klayton watercolor—let's see, that was his house gift four years ago— should probably be moved from the guest bathroom to the entrance way, though it does match the new marble tiles perfectly, and goodness, we can't forget to bring his wife's multicolored, jelly-bean platter down from the attic, though we still aren't sure Janine didn't mean it as a joke. And we must call the art restorer to see if he's replaced the matting on the Binner, since they're good friends of the Horstels, and we must also ask if he was able to disinfect the canvas so there is no hint of Nero's recurring bladder problem; it proved so ruinous to the Mendoza triptych that we can only dine out with them, and of course pick up the check, year after year after year.

And by the way, his wife said, the Hampton Art Museum called to remind us that we still haven't retrieved the Missy Massey painting that we'd donated to their auction last year. We told her we were donating it, so heaven forbid she asks what it went for. The director suggested that requiring the opening bid begin at $200 might have been a bit high. Surely, her husband said wistfully, someone might be at this year's art auction who really loves Peoria, as in *I 'heart' Peoria*, since the Finleys have stopped speaking to us ever since Finn found his *I 'heart' Frogs* behind the ficus in the library. Or was it in the closet?

What is this anyway, his wife said, why can't our artist friends arrive with two exquisite ripe cheeses? Or, he said, a vintage Bordeaux or a good bottle of champagne—house gifts, they agreed, that would disappear at evening's end into the Hamptons' own starry night.

IV.
A Multitude of Rhythms

If we split the basic two-part sequence in half, we get four parts instead: A, B, C, and D. Many Americans who came of age during the second half of the twentieth century are familiar with the standardized aptitude tests which, like hurdles on a racetrack, we had to undergo during our educational careers. And one part of these, for many years, was a section where one had to pick, out of several possibilities, the best entry for the fourth part of a double-paired analogy: given the first pair—A:B—choose the word or phrase that best transfers the relationship from C . . . D_1, D_2, D_3, or D_4. For example: *circle* is to *sphere* as *square* is to *cube, balloon, pentagon,* or *pendragon?*

But any series of four parts, like the simple time signature 4/4 at the beginning of a piece of music, has a multitude of rhythms one can dance to.

Mary E. Wilkins (1852–1930)[23]

PASTELS IN PROSE

In the Marsh-Land

Far over in the east is the marsh-land. Naught passes through it but the wind—the wind bent on strange ends—or a bird winged and swift, like a soul; but there are no souls in the marsh-land.

No foot of man sounds the deep pools; no boat cleaves the thick grasses. The pools gleam red; the grass is coarse and thick as the hair of a goat; it is flung here and there in shaggy fleeces tinged with red, as if from slaughter. Over in the east the sun stands low; his red rays color the mist like wine. The flags threaten in the wind like spears, but no heroes wield them.

There is no man in the marsh-land, in whose deep pools could be found death, whose thick grasses could moor a boat forever. It is a lonely place, and only my thought is there, striving to possess it all with wide vision.

Over the marsh-land stray odors from border flowers, but there is no sense to harbor them. Over the marsh-land the sound-waves float, but there is no tongue to awaken them to speech and no ear to receive them. In the marsh-land is God, without the souls in which alone He shines unto His own vision; in the marsh-land is God, a light without His own darkness.

The marsh-land is a lonely place; there is no man there. Only my thought is there, holding what it can encompass of God.

Camilla's Snuff-Box

Here is Camilla's snuff-box.

There were shouts in the street, and the torches flared. Camilla was borne along in her sedan-chair to the rout. Her delicate yellow face, as full of fine lines as a Chinese ivory carving, was seen through the window. She wore a velvet turban, and her head nodded ever as if in a wind.

The bearers shouted; the torches flared; red flames flickered in rosy smoke. Camilla was borne along to the rout in her sedan-chair.

Camilla opened her snuff box; her slender fingers, pointed like ivory bodkins, stirred up the pungent snuff; her nostrils were as fine and fleshless as old ivory.

Camilla's time of love was past; she went to the rout with only painted roses in her cheeks, and she took a pinch of snuff.

The bearers shouted; the night was full of dark winds, which bent the red flames of the torches.

Camilla's snuff-box was of fine silver-work, and her name was on the lid. Her lover had given it to her; but her lover was long since dead, and the memory of his kisses no longer made her heart sweet.

Camilla was old, and her time of love was past. She took a pinch of snuff from her silver snuff-box, as she went to the rout in her sedan-chair, with her palsied head nodding like a Chinese toy in a cabinet.

The bearers shouted; but their shouts have long since died away. The night was full of dark winds; but the winds went down. Long ago the torches burnt out. Long ago Camilla went no more to routs, her head ceased nodding, and her funeral procession went out of sight, in a black file, down the city street. Long ago Camilla's grave was forgotten, and there was no love left for her on the earth. But here is her snuff-box.

Shadows

The black dog runs across the meadow, with his shadow at his side as fleet as he. Let him speed as he may, he cannot outspeed his shadow. There is light in the world.

It is spring. The grass is young, and the west wind blows. The banks of the brook are yellow with cowslips. The grasses all lean east when the west wind blows, and their shadows overlie them. Now the cowslips darken under a shadow. There is light in the world.

The apple-trees cast their blossoms in their dark circles of shadow. The birds fly singing overhead, and their silent shadows glide beneath them over the meadow. There is light in the world.

Half the farm-house roof glistens in the morning sun, and half is purple with shadow. The shadow of the chimney smoke floats like a cloud, over the meadow. There is light in the world.

Anne stands in the doorway. Her yellow hair and her blue gown gleam true in clear light, but she thinks of her lover, and shadows follow her thoughts. "Oh, my lover has gone on a journey! Should he lose his way! Should thieves waylay him to harm him! Should his feet falter! Should evil befall him, my lover!"

Anne stands in the doorway. Her yellow hair and her blue gown gleam true in clear light, but her thoughts cast shadows. There is love in her heart.

Death

There is a little garden full of white flowers before this house, before this little house, which is sunken in a green hillock to the lintel of its door. The white flowers are full of honey; yellow butterflies and bees suck at them. The unseen wind comes rushing like a presence and a power which the heart feels only. The white flowers press together before it in a soft tumult, and shake out fragrance like censers; but the bees and the butterflies cling to them blowing. The crickets chirp in the green roof of the house unceasingly, like clocks which have told off the past, and will tell off the future.

I pray you, friend, who dwells in this little house sunken in the green hillock, with the white flower garden before the door?

A dead man.

Passes he ever out of his little dwelling and down the path between his white flower-bushes?

He never passes out.

There is no chimney in that grassy roof. How fares he when the white flowers are gone and the white storm drives?

He feels it not.

Had he happiness?

His heart broke for it.

Does his heart pain him in there?

He has forgot.

Comes ever anybody here to visit him?

His widow comes in her black veil, and weeps here, and sometimes his old mother, wavering out in the sun like a black shadow.

And he knows it not?

He knows it not.

He knows not of his little prison-house in the green hillock, of his white flower-garden, of the winter storm, of his broken heart, and his beloved who yet bear the pain of it, and send out their thoughts to watch with him in the wintry nights?

He knows it not.

Only the living know?

Only the living.

Then, then the tombs be not for the dead, but the living! I would, I would, I would that I were dead, that I might be free from the tomb, and sorrow, and death!

Emily Holmes Coleman (1899–1974)[24]

THE WREN'S NEST

When over the highway and through the brush a tramp on the wind came lightly sighing then into the lane down the trodden periwinkles shuddering between forced stones fled the captive and after her the futile trailing of her long red skirt. She sang up to the wren's nests and built for herself on the stone wall a house of bark and silence.

His eyes were waterfalls over the rocks and from his chin went out assurance of desire. They had come together on the hill where the cows went astray and he had seen her with her long branched stick chasing them back into the valley. She jumped on the back of one and it ran sinking to the stream. Down to the stream they had gone and their feet had chiseled its depth. They stood making rivulets through the dam and lay on the bank in the sun with his hat over her eyes and his arm across her breast. The cows wandered up the hill again and in the stinking sun they lashed the great flies and chewed their contemplation beneath the trees.

Come on with me. We must while them home now and you can meet my mother. His hair wet from the stream had dried, and in the slumber of summer his ears and cheeks had gone wet and his hair above his ears was coiled in small turnings. I cannot stand that, she said to him, come with me and put on your hat. I have to go back to the city he told her.

In the evening she sat out on the porch and listened for the whippoorwills. He had shyly eaten their supper and afterwards bidden her mother a courteous goodbye. He had fastened her hand to his breast outside and gone gleaming down the dust to the village where the trains left for the large cities.

A nice young man, her mother called, come back in here why dont you, its cooler in here. She went in and sat in the dusk by the cold stove. If only you hadnt married said her mother you might have had him just think of it. I dont care she said I dont want him. She took her mothers hands and sang softly to her cap.

Well thats all there is to romance said her father at the breakfast table when the syrup glued out of the pot and from up the round soft bakings came flavor of buckwheat and sun.

In after years when the early winter winds pinched the trees and made of red and gold a barren silence she put on a coat of blue and caught up her skirt in the mirror. All there is for me to do is to walk like this and it can be done. Her hat fitted snugly and the feather was bright red. You will come back said her mother you will find that the cows cannot go alone.

You see that he doesnt let them wander in the sun said she deftly and pressing finely her mothers face. You will all be quiet and when I return there will be mourning. Into the buggy she stepped primly and waved a small white handkerchief to her mother on the porch. Go inside you will catch something there because the wind is coming.

The train screamed on frenzied wings through the green and out over the water and in again to trees. She sat with her bag above her head and her knees folded over. The woman across the aisle lived in many places and had come from Europe that day. She gave her a little pin of violet to look in and see the European cities. If she would not like me I could think my thoughts. In the brown meadows, touched with green, there were cows. They melted into the green and stood sighing beneath the trees.

She went out to the platform and stood alone from the woman and sped across the earth. Little houses of brick and sand muttered in the corners and fast through the afternoon went the train and fast into the night. Over the gulleys and swift into the sun and rattling across the iron bridges over the towns. It was coming fast, fast from the little houses, closer to the train and faster to the trees. It shattered and swung and lifted and rocked and fast into the city went the train. It was coming, it would be the end and she would stand alone and motionless upon the track. Are you coming? And the fast bled trees stood off their dull response.

Now into the city went the train and hushed from her eyes and bent her head. And crushed across the narrow streets on iron structure and poured hot fire into the shed at the end. This was the city he was shouting and the baggage was piled at the end. She leaped from her ears and quieted her hands with sorrow. She was to stand upon the curb and see people going to their places and speaking a foreign tongue.

✳   ✳   ✳

What do you think you can do here you had better go home and speak your piece. I dont care I shall stay anyway. It was with fervor and soft hands pressed against the glass.

You dont seem to realize he told her that anything so exquisite belongs in the sun and shade. Not here she said there is no sun. They sat drinking in a cold cafe and on the ground were sparrows jumping for the cheese. There were woodchucks and little wrens. All on the stone wall. Will you go to market in the morning and tell me what you find? No she said I am afraid you will be gone.

That settles it he said I will not have my will abrogated. She laughed against the frown on his white and famished brow.

So what more there is to do is hard to say. If you will consult your husband you may find that there is cause for your return. But I love your hair she said it flows over your head and you are not a boy. Go back he said it was not meant for you.

*   *   *

My mother can see that I have come back. Green in the damp and weltered in the marsh. For the apples I was gone, the apples sunk into the kettle and mashed. They were good in the jars. Thank you my mother your hair is of course not wet like his and silk and cold. But where is your husband she told her, you did not see him. Oh yes many things we talked and he has learned to love me. Then why didnt you bring him with you? I found him cold and interested in many vices.

Crowded into the memories of the winter came the spring, warm in the swamps and drying. She sat along the stone walls with her stick and pushed them into ponds for her desire. Will you go back from me she fiercely shouted to the sun and went violently up the lane behind him. She struck from her hand the stick and made pools in the mud of love and vengeance. She built cities in the wood and crossed twigs over their depths and sang. Now chocolate for the horses of the Tsar they will be calling for them. She hitched golden horses to the old carriage of her impotence and they stood champing and did not run away. Over the bars it would come and out rattling to the highway, dragged behind him. She went softly up behind the bull and poked him with her stick. He leaned to one side and nosed in the ground. She poked him again on his white and listless flank and he sprang quivering

57

on his feet and turned to poise his head. Into the ground went bellowing his clotted hoof, pawing not grimly and leaning to one side. Under his head all fury and design and lurching to her his trembling legs. She advanced an inch and poked his light nostril and stood lilting to the fence. Down with his snorting went the wind and over to her place went fury belching bull head in restraint and tail high on the wind. Close to her smell came bent and perching head and over the fence went she with grace of flouting spring. He came up short where she had leaped and backed and belched and gouged upon the bars his sharp tined horns made havoc in the logs.

Enough for you she cried with pointed stick go back lie down under the sun and gouge again the pails made of cardboard.

David Young (1936–   )[25]

FOUR ABOUT HEAVY MACHINERY

A huge cement truck turns the corner, and you get the full impact of its sensuality. Those ruts in the road or on the lawn! Even at night the cement plant has a strange energy, drawing adolescents to stare through its fences, causing the watchman to shine his light nervously among the parked and sleeping mixers. Still, from those fluid beginnings and slow revolutions, the cement itself forms the pale and stony squares of side-walk. Reassuring. Roller skates, hopscotch, salted ice. Then the slow cracking from the tree roots below and we are bade to sensuality again.

*   *   *

Cranes are not to be compared with trees, not with their almost Scandinavian sense of the importance of duty and power. Sometimes the face is very far from the heart, and the one thing you would like to do—lie down next to that beautiful passing stranger, for instance—is the thing that seems least possible. So you sway against the gray sky, pretending to a stiffness you do not feel. The building you helped create rises toward you, filled with the sounds of hammering and the strange shine of work-lights.

*   *   *

To take some tutoring from pumps, I said. I was thinking about the windmill, that swaying, clanking lecturer. Slow cows come to drink from the tank. We filled it, didn't we, harvesting water from weather, not by bringing it down from the sky like rain, but up from the earth like oil. Now roll up your blue sleeve and plunge your arm into that tank. If you clench and unclench your fist regularly you can learn something about the submersible pump, beating down there where weather is a dream.

*   *   *

We have strong feelings about bulldozers, their buzzing and scraping, their clumsy abruptness, their way of tipping saplings into piles of burnable roots and brush. Our faces get vinegary when we think of it. But the bulldozer's point of view is remarkably different. The bulldozer thinks of itself as a lover. It considers that its loved one, from whom it is always separated, is wrapped in many short, soft, buttery strips of leather. It imagines itself removing these worn leather wrappings, one at a time and with great tenderness, to get at the body of the loved one. Perverse, you will say. But see, you have already entered the life of the bulldozer: your hands reach for the next piece of leather. Shrubs and young trees go under.

Amy Knox Brown (1961–   )[26]

FOUR EPISODES IN THE LIFE
OF THE SHERIDAN BOULEVARD TROLL

1. After Drinking Two Bottles of Night Train, the Troll beneath the Sheridan Boulevard Bridge in Lincoln, Nebraska, Awakens to the Sounds of Goats

The troll opens his eyes. He lies next to a culvert. Rocks rattle in his head, the taste of sulfur fills his mouth.

Overhead, a bell rings again and again.

The troll curls his fingers around the spindly trunks of volunteer trees to haul himself up the incline and onto the bridge.

He sees a goat—so young that his horns are only tiny mounds on his skull—riding an old Schwinn. Screwed to the handlebars is one of those little bells the goat strikes his hoof against again and again. The sound penetrates the troll's skull like a blade.

The sound must stop.

The troll lurches toward the bicycle. The goat's eyes widen and he veers around the troll, looking back as he rides away, still ringing the godforsaken bell.

In the park on the other side of the bridge, children scream.

The troll has an intimation that things will get worse before they get better. He sinks down against the bridge's railings and rests his head in his hands.

Along comes a second goat, this one larger and older than the little one, riding a cream-colored Vespa.

The thought of cream nauseates the troll. He stands. The clouds overhead part and a spear of sunlight cuts into the troll's face. The goat is singing, loudly and off key, a song about not getting any satisfaction.

The troll thinks he needs to kill the goat. He'll kill the goat, stop the singing, and sell the scooter for Mad Dog.

He heads toward the Vespa, his hairy hands outstretched to grab.

The goat—the insolent, adolescent goat—looks right at the troll and sneers. He yells out, "And I try, and I try—" and then shoots away along Sheridan Boulevard, leaving the troll in a puff of exhaust.

The troll coughs. He doubles over. He thinks of the phrase "coughing up a lung." That's what it feels like he's doing. He wonders if he's going to die.

Maybe this is the *worst* part. Black dots swim in front of his eyes.

From the park comes a noise that sounds as if one of the children is hitting the pole of a swing set with a crowbar. And then, a moment of reprieve: the crowbar sound stops, a cloud covers the sun, the troll finds himself able to breathe again.

He straightens. In the gutter, he sees a half-smoked Marlboro someone tossed from a passing car. He lifts the cigarette to his lips. He tastes the lipstick of the previous smoker. He thinks of the phrase "hair of the dog." But then, from the west, a police car rolls up and parks. The driver is a goat in an officer's uniform. He wears sunglasses, so you can't see his eyes, but the troll expects they hold no mercy.

The police goat steps out of the car. He taps his billy-club against his palm. Sounds bleat from the scanner, a jumble of words that might be in a foreign language, because the troll doesn't understand a single one of them. The police goat smiles, showing yellow teeth, and the troll understands that the worst is yet to come.

2. Friendly Bearers of Salvation A and B

A. The troll lies under the Sheridan Boulevard bridge, beaten—badly beaten—but not dead. His eyes are closed. His fingers twitch, long nails digging divots in the earth. A hot wind washes over him.

In the distance, the bells toll from the Cathedral of the Risen Christ. It must be Sunday. Or it might be Saturday, or some Holy Day. The troll opens his eyes to see—or does he open his eyes to see?—a nun approaching. Wind swirls the skirt of her seersucker habit and curls the edges of her wimple. Her pupils are vertical lines in her golden eyes. Her face appears to be covered with soft gray fur. In one hand she holds a chalice, in the other a round wafer the size of a quarter.

She places the wafer in the troll's mouth. She tells him to raise his head. Can't, he says.

Yes, you can. You have to try.

He lifts his head. She places one hand against the back of his neck to hold him steady, tips the chalice against his lips, and fills his mouth with blood.

B. The troll lies under the bridge, staring at the vertical lines of the concrete pillars. From a nearby tree, a squirrel drops acorns that smack into the troll's open palms.

Who are you? asks the squirrel.

The troll considers. *Trip trap*, he replies. *Trip, trap*, whispers the bridge. *Trip, trap.*

3. Forgive Us the Trespassers

Sister Mary Frances was walking across the Sheridan Boulevard bridge at 11:50 p.m. on Monday, June 21, 1981, when she heard glass shatter against the joists beneath her feet. Bursts of light rose from under the bridge. At the scene, officers found tracks leading down the embankment: sole prints from Converse tennis shoes, as well as small divots that appeared to have been made by hooves.

Against the west bridge abutment lay shards of glass from mercury bulbs that, according to a janitor at Lincoln Southeast High School (three blocks east), had been deposited in the outdoor trash bin on the afternoon of Monday, June 21.

The railroad tracks under the bridge still held some heat from the Burlington Northern, which passed through at 11:30 p.m.

On the ground by the east bridge abutment lay five empty Falstaff cans.

A homeless man nearby was drinking from a can of Falstaff. He claimed he'd seen nothing unusual; he'd found the Falstaff on the ground; the can was still cold.

Approximately fifty yards from the bridge, three billy-goats grazed. Animal Control was called, but the goats absconded, running south, before Animal Control officers arrived.

The janitor explained that, when the mercury bulbs were broken, the small amount of gas inside them ignited and produced a burst of fire.

Sister Mary Frances believed she'd seen the work of the Devil.

A trail of Falstaff cans (some still containing beer, which officers poured on the railroad tracks) led south along the tracks and up the incline toward 33rd Street.

Questioned again, the homeless man repeated that he'd seen nothing unusual. He said he wanted to clarify that he wasn't homeless, that he was a troll, and that the bridge was his home.

One officer explained that the bridge, in fact, belonged to the city of Lincoln.

The troll shrugged.

Another officer followed the trail of Falstaff cans, which ended at 33rd Street. He reported hearing laughter in the distance (the laughter, he thought, of teenage boys), as well as bleating that sounded like goats.

4. A Christmas Story

December arrives, that month of blood and ice. Snow coats the streets, piles on the pillars of the Sheridan Boulevard bridge, melts on the lashes of carolers whose words of Holy Nights and King Wenceslas freeze when leaving their mouths and drop like teeth into the snow.

Under the bridge, the troll builds a fire. Flames glint cheerfully on the broken shards of Night Train bottles around him. He can barely hear the carolers. He is warm enough.

A trio of goats has been seen around town, as far away as Havelock, where they trip-trap past the window of Arnold's Bar, startling the railway workers who've stopped for beer after work. There are three goats: a little one, a middle-sized one, and a big one with evil-looking horns. For years, the men who see the goats will argue about the size of the horns, the order in which the goats passed the window, what each goat meant. Over the years, the stories change. The stories grow. In the stories, the goats live on, forever.

The nuns outside the Cathedral of the Risen Christ wear their black winter habits under their black winter coats.

On the snowy park ground, a black squirrel slices through the whiteness like an exclamation point. It is said that black squirrels mean change. We want to know what kind of change is coming. We lock our doors.

The smell of wood smoke and meat rises from under the Sheridan Boulevard Bridge. O my pretty ones, let us step closer and see what the troll is roasting over his little fire. As we descend the incline, our feet leave no tracks in the snow. Our breath does not cloud in the air as the carolers' does when they pass overhead, singing.

The troll sits on his haunches, sheltered from the inclement weather by the bridge, which stretches overhead like the sky. He wears a plush Santa hat, a gift from one of those boys who goes under the bridge to drink Falstaff and break things. The troll radiates the kind of contentment you see in someone fishing; he's transfixed by his yellow flames, the quiet sound of falling snow that will not touch him. He nudges the object he is roasting with a stick.

We see that the roasting object is an animal. It is, in fact, a goat. But which goat? We step closer. The troll adjusts his rudimentary spit and prods again to see if the meat is done, and we can tell, now, that he's roasting the largest of the three goats once seen running around town, the goat some gullible children had mistaken for a reindeer because of its horns.

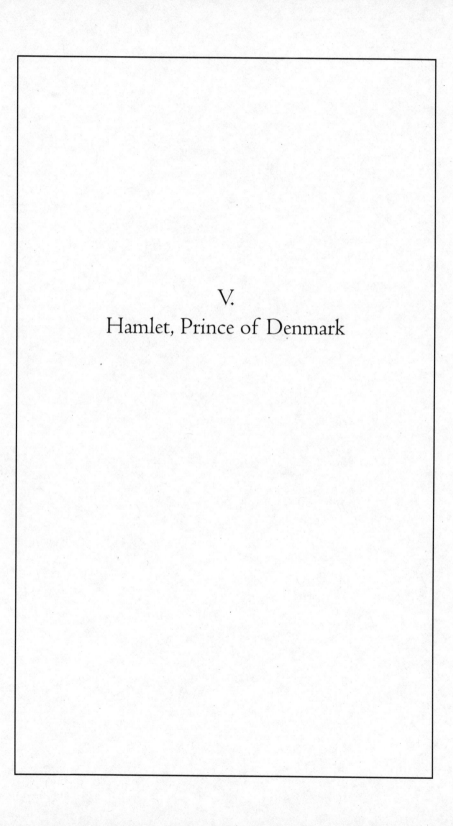

V.

Hamlet, Prince of Denmark

For one possible five-part structure we have to look no further than Shakespeare's tragedies. How many generations of college students, do you suppose, have been confronted by the task of writing a paper on "the five-part rising and falling action of *King Lear*?" Or again, how many Sunday afternoons, with the TV blaring football from the living-room, has a student searched the Internet for a paper he or she can submit on "the five-part structure of *Hamlet, Prince of Denmark*"?—as though the tortured soul himself can be dismembered into five interlinked pieces.

But forget drama. Far more mundane, if that's possible, are the thousands of pentalogical "themes" that students have had to write in so-called composition classes—with some skeletal instruction manual to guide them in the process: First, synopsize what you're going to write about; then, in three parts—introduction, evidence, and conclusion—prove your point (with specific details, *please!*); then wrap it all up with a summary of what you've just accomplished—or failed to accomplish—and if you're really avant-garde, you might want to give some indication of its importance to the broader world of sex, drugs, and rock'n'roll. Which is to say that a five-part structure is just an expanded three-part model, but in this case—beginning, middle, and end—the middle has three parts of its own.

Fortunately there are a myriad of other possibilities from which writers (and readers) can choose.

Dora Greenwell McChesney (1871–1912)[27]

AT OLD ITALIAN CASEMENTS

From a Tuscan Window

A high dark Florentine palace with frowning cornice and barred windows, rich torch-holders of wrought iron set beside the deep-arched doorway. In one of the casements stands a young girl; it is early morning and the fresh light shines over her. She has been, perhaps, at a banquet, for she is in gala dress—soft green worked with threads of silver; about her slim long throat is a chain with an ornament of enamel bright with shifting colors. She grasps the heavy iron with a small white hand and leans forward; the shadow of one bar lies like a dark band across the bright hair drawn smoothly back from her forehead. She is watching for her lover to pass in the dusky street; her lips are grave, but there is a smile in the brown eyes under the fine curved brows. She looks out through the sunrise and waits. Underneath the window, so close to the wall that he cannot be seen from above, lies a youth wrapped in a dark mantle—dead—he has been stabbed there in the night and fallen quite silently. His loose dark hair brushes the ground where he lies; his blood has made a stain on the grey stones. His white face is turned up; his eyes are open, looking towards the casement— the casement where the maiden leans, watching for her lover to pass in the sunrise.

In the Palace of the Duke

The window is wreathed about with strange carvings, where mocking faces look from among the vines. Against the broad sill a youth is leaning, looking into the court below where his horse is being led out and his falconer is waiting. The lad is dressed with great richness, his close crimson doublet and hosen curiously slashed and his short cloak thick with golden embroidery. His dark hair makes a cloud about a delicate willful face. In one hand he holds a casket of amber wrought with the loves of the gods, and before him on the ledge lie papers newly signed. Close by him are two figures; a man still young and a stately woman whose hair is grey beneath her jeweled head-dress and veil. They are mother and son, for their features are alike, and wasted alike before the time by some long hunger of desire. She has her left hand on her bosom, pressed hard almost as though on something hidden there; with her right she holds a goblet of silver to the youth, who reaches backwards for it, not turning, with an indolent gesture. He glances carelessly to the court below, but the eyes of mother and son have met, unflinchingly, in a slow smile of terrible understanding.

A Venetian Balcony

Night on the waters, yet no darkness. On the still lagoons broad sheen of moonlight; in the canals and squares of Venice shifting and dashing lights of many lamps and torches, for it is a night of festival. From a balcony set with discs of alabaster, purple and white, a woman is bending to look across the water. She is full in the mingling of lights, white of the moonbeams, gold of the wide-flaring torches; they shine on the warm whiteness of brow and throat and bosom and the gold of her hair which she wears coiled high, like a crown, about a jeweled dagger. She holds her mask in her left hand on which is no ring. There is a smile on her proud lips, but the great fire of her eyes is dying; into the triumph is stealing a touch of fear and the sense of a woman's first surrender. The night is all but gone, the revelry at its close. She looks across the water where the moon has made a silver track, but her eyes seek only the track of a gondola which has passed— slipped from her sight. Back in the dusk rich room a single silver lamp is burning; it throws a gleam on her own picture. A master hand has set her there as the holy Saint Catherine, robed like a queen, as indeed she is this night, but kneeling humbly before the Blessed Babe and holding a spousal ring.

A Brother of St. Francis

Low and narrow, the window of a convent cell, but it commands the width of Umbrian plain, above which the sun is scarcely risen. A great band of saffron light outlines the far horizon, but the full day has not come. Close to the walls of the cloister rise slender trees, shooting up as if athirst for the sun, their tall stems bare and straight, only breaking at the top into leafage. These lift a delicate tracery of green against the rose-grey of the sky, but, beyond, the lower slopes are dim with the ashen mist of the olives. And still beyond the plain sweeps out, showing no wood or stream, making ready wide barren spaces to be touched into beauty by the changing sky. The sun has hardly given full life to the colors beneath; the green and yellow and grey merge tremulously. The virginal air of early dawn is not yet brushed away. The plain lies dream-like—rapt in a great expectancy. From the casement a young monk looks out. He wears the brown habit of a Franciscan. His eyes are wide and fixed and he looks into the sunrise and beyond it. His face is worn and very pale, so that the early light seems to shine through it, meeting a light from within; his lips are parted, not in prayer but in some breathless rapture of contemplation. The morning brightness searches his barren cell, touches his coarse garments and his clasped hands. The marks of fast and vigil are upon him. In his face is the fullness of utter renunciation—and the peace of a great promise. Outside, above the narrow window of his cell, the mated birds are building.

The Cardinal's Outlook

Wide splendor of the sunset beating down upon Rome; the statues on column and church front stand aloof, and uplifted in the red glow the dark shafts of the cypresses are kindled by it into dusky gold. It shines in at the window where the Cardinal is sitting and dwells on his rich robes—then is subdued and lost in the room behind. Yet even there fugitive gleams respond to it, from rare enamel and wrought metal; most of all from the statuette of a Bacchante, the golden bronze of which seems to hold the sun-rays. The ivory crucifix looks wan beside it. The Cardinal does not see the sunset, though a bar of brightness lies across the book open before him on which his left hand is pressed. The window is not all in light; outside, against the pageant of the sky rises a mighty bulk of darkness. It is the dome of St. Peter's. Its shadow lies across the Cardinal's dwelling and across the world of his thought. And there—close to the base of that dome, there in the heart of the Vatican, the Pope is dying. The Cardinal, new come from his bedside, sits waiting: soon the last mystic sacraments must be bestowed, soon the last throb of life must pass. He waits. He does not see the sunset; he sees instead the kneeling forms round the death-bed; he sees the shrouded halls and solemn gatherings of the Conclave. He sees—beyond—a mystery of ever widening domination, at the center of which is enthroned—not the old man who is dying yonder. Whose will it be—the solitary sovereign figure, soon to stand there where the dome rises and the great shadow lies? The Cardinal's face has grown sharp and sunken in these hours; it is of a pallor like the ivory crucifix behind him. Round his lips lingers the unchanging inward smile of priesthood. His eyes beneath their drooping lids are intent— patient—menacing. His right hand is a little lifted with an unconscious movement of benediction: with such a gesture it is that the Pope—from above the portico of the Lateran—blesses the kneeling multitudes.

Amy Lowell (1874–1925)[28]

SPRING DAY

Bath

The day is fresh-washed and fair, and there is a smell of tulips and narcissus in the air.

The sunshine pours in at the bath-room window and bores through the water in the bath-tub in lathes and planes of greenish-white. It cleaves the water into flaws like a jewel, and cracks it to bright light.

Little spots of sunshine lie on the surface of the water and dance, dance, and their reflections wobble deliciously over the ceiling; a stir of my finger sets them whirring, reeling. I move a foot, and the planes of light in the water jar. I lie back and laugh, and let the green-white water, the sun-flawed beryl water, flow over me. The day is almost too bright to bear, the green water covers me from the too bright day. I will lie here awhile and play with the water and the sun spots.

The sky is blue and high. A crow flaps by the window, and there is a whiff of tulips and narcissus in the air.

Breakfast Table

In the fresh-washed sunlight, the breakfast table is decked and white. It offers itself in flat surrender, tendering tastes, and smells, and colors, and metals, and grains, and the white cloth falls over its side, draped and wide. Wheels of white glitter in the silver coffee-pot, hot and spinning like catherine-wheels, they whirl, and twirl—and my eyes begin to smart, the little white, dazzling wheels prick them like darts. Placid and peaceful, the rolls of bread spread themselves in the sun to bask. A stack of butter-pats, pyramidal, shout orange through the white, scream, flutter, call: "Yellow! Yellow! Yellow!" Coffee steam rises in a stream, clouds the silver tea-service with mist, and twists up into the sunlight, revolved, involuted, suspiring higher and higher, fluting in a thin spiral up the high blue sky. A crow flies by and croaks at the coffee steam. The day is new and fair with good smells in the air.

Walk

Over the street the white clouds meet, and sheer away without touching.

On the sidewalks, boys are playing marbles. Glass marbles, with amber and blue hearts, roll together and part with a sweet clashing noise. The boys strike them with black and red striped agates. The glass marbles spit crimson when they are hit, and slip into the gutters under rushing brown water. I smell tulips and narcissus in the air, but there are no flowers anywhere, only white dust whipping up the street, and a girl with a gay Spring hat and blowing skirts. The dust and the wind flirt at her ankles and her neat, high-heeled patent leather shoes. Tap, tap, the little heels pat the pavement, and the wind rustles among the flowers on her hat.

A water-cart crawls slowly on the other side of the way. It is green and gay with new paint, and rumbles contentedly, sprinkling clear water over the white dust. Clear zigzagging water, which smells of tulips and narcissus.

The thickening branches make a pink *grisaille* against the blue sky.

Whoop! The clouds go dashing at each other and sheer away just in time. Whoop! And a man's hat careers down the street in front of the white dust, leaps into the branches of a tree, veers away and trundles ahead of the wind, jarring the sunlight into spokes of rose-color and green.

A motor-car cuts a swathe through the bright air, sharp-beaked, irresistible, shouting to the wind to make way. A glare of dust and sunshine tosses together behind it, and settles down. The sky is quiet and high, and the morning is fair with fresh-washed air.

Midday and Afternoon

Swirl of crowded streets. Shock and recoil of traffic. The stock-still brick façade of an old church, against which the waves of people lurch and withdraw. Flare of sunshine down side-streets. Eddies of light in the windows of chemists' shops, with their blue, gold, purple jars, darting colors far into the crowd. Loud bangs and tremors, murmurings out of high windows, whirring of machine belts, blurring of horses and motors. A quick spin and shudder of brakes on an electric car, and the jar of a church-bell knocking against the metal blue of the sky. I am a piece of the town, a bit of blown dust, thrust along with the crowd. Proud to feel the pavement under me, reeling with feet. Feet tripping, skipping, lagging, dragging, plodding doggedly, or springing up and advancing on firm elastic insteps. A boy is selling papers, I smell them clean and new from the press. They are fresh like the air, and pungent as tulips and narcissus.

The blue sky pales to lemon, and great tongues of gold blind the shop-windows, putting out their contents in a flood of flame.

Night and Sleep

The day takes her ease in slippered yellow. Electric signs gleam out along the shop fronts, following each other. They grow, and grow, and blow into patterns of fire-flowers as the sky fades. Trades scream in spots of light at the unruffled night. Twinkle, jab, snap, that means a new play; and over the way: plop, drop, quiver, is the sidelong sliver of a watchmaker's sign with its length on another street. A gigantic mug of beer effervesces to the atmosphere over a tall building, but the sky is high and has her own stars, why should she heed ours?

I leave the city with speed. Wheels whirl to take me back to my trees and my quietness. The breeze which blows with me is fresh-washed and clean, it has come but recently from the high sky. There are no flowers in bloom yet, but the earth of my garden smells of tulips and narcissus.

My room is tranquil and friendly. Out of the window I can see the distant city, a band of twinkling gems, little flower-heads with no stems. I cannot see the beer-glass, nor the letters of the restaurants and shops I passed, now the signs blur and all together make the city, glowing on a night of fine weather, like a garden stirring and blowing for the Spring.

The night is fresh-washed and fair and there is a whiff of flowers in the air.

Wrap me close, sheets of lavender. Pour your blue and purple dreams into my ears. The breeze whispers at the shutters and mutters queer tales of old days, and cobbled streets, and youths leaping their horses down marble stairways. Pale blue lavender, you are the color of the sky when it is fresh-washed and fair . . . I smell the stars . . . they are like tulips and narcissus . . . I smell them in the air.

Robert Duncan (1919–1988)[29]

CONCERNING THE MAZE

We were surrounded at that time by avenues of escape. You began at a certain point and went on, and the streets were the natural runways where we tried the same turn over and over again being lost in the maze. Where only a second before someone had passed before us we could smell fear and confusion in their sweat along the walls.

One of us got a dry section of cheese by running the right angle and then twice to the left. He tried it again and found the same dry section of cheese. One ran down past three bypaths, turned the circle, went down instead of up and found a hole gnawed in the wood. He went through, out into the world on the other side of the sky. Others have crouched at that crack in the wall entangled in wire, pissing with fear, seeing only the glassy reflection of their own eyes on the other side.

*   *   *

If we always had found food there, and then there was no food, if then there is never any food there where we had expected to find food: there are definite somatic results that such a frustration has on us. We lose sleep. Our hair grows thick with secretions and coarse and scarce with age. Our skin is scaly. And we are given to tremens.

It is even more horrible when we can find no doors.

*   *   *

We kept seeing that there was a certain way to get at the food. It was very simple. We could all see that—that it must be very simple, a very very simple thing, an everyday thing that any one of us could do. There were only a given number of things among which we could choose: jump onto the little platform, roll the wooden ball down the groove, turn to the right and pull the latch, run up the inclined plane and jump into the net, make a dive for the door at the far corner of the room. But only one of these was the correct choice. Any one thing, if it were wrong, would set into motion a cycle of events which might never lead us back to an opportunity, back to the GREAT OPPORTUNITY which we now faced. It was very simple, however. It was OBVIOUS that one of these things—maybe rolling the wooden ball down the groove—would bring freedom. It was surely a very commonplace thing, some one of these simple acts that any of us, as I have said before, could do to release himself. Some of us had made the choice before and run wild to come again and again to this same place, but we could not remember what we had chosen—the trials that had resulted from that choice had been so severe. I only want to tell something about the choice. It is a simple thing to jump onto the platform and find out, to roll the wooden ball down the groove and find out, to run up the inclined plane and jump and find out, to turn to the right and release the latch and find out, to make a dash for the door and find out. But we remember the ordeals of the years that come from a wrong choice, and we have returned here so many times that we cannot remember what choices we have made that were wrong. It seems as if all of them are wrong, and yet we know that that is not so. There is one right way. There is only that way, we know that there is a way we have not tried before, one which will save us, but we have gone thru so many errors that we cannot be sure that any given act might not be a repeated error.

It is so simple. A choice among five acts. Yet some have died of exhaustion. And it is hunger not over-eating that gives us nightmares.

*   *   *

Parables are partly true.

*   *   *

There was a long narrow tunnel or a hall cut into a great block of stone with barely enough room for two to pass if they stood sideways against the walls, and I was running on a treadmill there. Far down the hall I could see a man standing in the white light of a doorway. There was a fire inside the room behind him of burning newspaper, never consumed. I could see this man standing, and I was conscious that I was very young and that the treadmill would go on forever. I remembered the horses, white and gawdy with ribbons that raced on the yellow treadmill in the circus. I raced on and on. L'idée fixe. I raced on and on. I could see this man standing, peering down the hall at me, miles down the hall; a great white light was all around him so that he stood black in the center of a white light that ran out like water over the sand of the floor, and I could hear all around us the terrific breathing of the sea. I noticed that the walls at my side were moist and salty. A coating of mucous surrounded me, loading me down as I struggled to move down the hall, my hoofs kicking out over the treadmill. The man standing at the door so far away couldn't see who I was. If I could only come near enough for him to recognize me, the problem of the foodtrap would be solved. At that moment I realized that the tunnel was under water. There was a rusty puddle all about me, and the treadmill had become clogged with sand and rubbish of shells and weeds washed in by the tides. I ran on and on down the long tunnel, knowing that I would drown when I reached the light.

Carol Guess (1968–)[30]

REVIVAL OF ROSEMALING

The Ruined Garden

Everyone lost someone in the avalanche that year. Nights, we held dances in the ruined garden. Wolves wove the trail but stopped short of the fireline. The mountain refused to name what it knew. When a dog, child, or mitten went missing we wore miner's headlamps, bright sieves for thick dark. Everyone waltzed, but not everyone tangoed. Hard-packed snow tumbled, gathering speed, eating ice farmers, sentries, and skis. We shouted questions, but our questions stirred rocks. We had to learn not to talk—to move mutely, we of the valley—and to bury the bodies when spring thawed ice walls. Our dead came down perfect, red in their cheeks, palms flexed as if resisting the pyre.

Marietta

No one knew about the cabin. People thought I lived in town in a wooden house with a bright red door. No one had ever seen the house because the house wasn't real. I lived in a cabin on the outskirts of town. I had to haul my garbage to the dump. When someone got hurt, the ambulance came from somewhere else. No one could see the cabin from the road, although I could see the road and the bay. No one could see what I was doing or who I was with. All winter, snow kept the shape of snow, sirens muffled, Amtrak derailed. Llamas stumbled into the field and slept standing up, manes brittle with frost. Once a hawk flew into the window. Once you dressed me up as a boy. Once you came home in a stranger's coat and shook strange snow onto the concrete floor.

Crown Hill

Stairs spiraled up to an attic filled with salt. We slept thin as tripwire, taut among pillows. One night strangers stared down through the skylight. Glass divided stage from audience. What we wanted was applause. We showed them everything, and when it rained they never went home again. Our hands signed the story of what it meant to be warm.

Field

We fled the city at night. I was distracted by your body. My suitcase chipped at the bone in my thigh. Thieves stole doorways and sold them to trees, scrubby oaks that grew up on the street. Beyond the factory we slept in a field littered with swan's-down, beer husks, and bees. We fed a fire to blister coyotes. We strung death along on thinness alone.

Museum

The house that lived beside us is gone, replaced by concrete for a three-car garage. At the estate sale, dealers priced Norwegian dolls. We saved a squirrel from a tangle of chard. Maybe charm got confused with harm by someone like me or maybe by me. We chipped ice from bootprints to brew into tea. What did we know of strangeness? What might've saved us lived somewhere else. We hung aces from trees axed for newfangled holidays. We knit shadows from snow, leading wolves to false prey.

VI.
A Graveyard of Forgotten Novels

When I began my doctoral research on the prose poem, my first impulse was to look for sequences. I haunted the stacks of Memorial Library at the University of Wisconsin, pulling books down off the shelves and examining their innards as if in haruspication of my future. There was no other way to identify what I was looking for, no reader's guide that pointed to prose poems. Likewise no catalog in existence listed prose according to whether or not its authors had divided their work into little pieces.

A friend of mine from the Netherlands told me how lucky I was, able to enter the stacks myself, whereas if I were doing this research in Europe I would be limited to giving little slips of paper with author and title information to other grad students, hired help who would retrieve the material from the stacks themselves—as I in fact needed to do here with books and literary magazines from the rare book collection. (Such was the innocence of the times that by the end of the school year the staff allowed me to ascend the rickety stairs to the old fire-proof vault and retrieve those books and magazines myself. That vault, and indeed the whole reading room and rare book department—to say nothing of the staff—have long since been replaced by more technologically-advanced individuals and systems.)

At that time, on the top floor of the north tower, so called, there was a room where I never saw another soul, where one could find books with the classification PZ (fiction in English), books that had not, through popularity or notoriety or mere critical acclaim or perhaps even sales numbers—I was never sure how they attained this status—ascended to the realm of PS or PN, American or English Literature. I would walk down the aisles, stopping almost at random (a familiar name here, a name that seemed like it should be familiar, there), opening books to see if the pages might perhaps be broken up into short sections, or whether, like most novels, the text blocks went from page to page, unbroken like a highway stretching out across a desert.

After a month or so of this increasingly-frustrating endeavor, with very little material to show for it, I stopped searching for novels-in-pieces. I decided, for the moment, to focus instead on collections of prose poems. For one thing, the shelves that contained poetry were less extensive (and the names far more familiar) than what I'd come to think of as the graveyard of forgotten novels—and so a random stack-crawl through poetry seemed far less daunting. Moreover, I could take a different tack and search for prose poems in the world-famous Memorial Library Little Magazine Collection, page by page and issue by issue—and in that way find authors whose books I could consult directly.

But it was in those first few weeks of picking books off shelves that I lost any impulse I still had to write a novel—or, as I told a colleague at the time, to have written a novel. Each of these books had had its moment, the dreams and fantasies of its author during the long days and nights of its conception and completion, its joyful day of acceptance and acquisition, its launch party, its postpartum life—and finally, after a year or two of mixed reviews and dismal sales, its appearance on remainder tables in the dim back-rooms of bookstores, and its ultimate deletion from the multi-volume (and now vanished) *Books in Print*.

At least, with a poem, each new beginning—and they could happen, with lyric poetry, once or even several times a day—each first line was another chance at a masterpiece, a piece that might live forever, anthologized to the last syllable of recorded time. And then a while later the initial draft would be done, and another one beckoned. But a novel could take years of work, and all the while the image of the graveyard of fiction, like the ghost at the banquet, hovered over one's writing table.

* * *

Nelson Algren — *Chicago: City on the Make*
Harry Crosby — *Sleeping Together*
Ben Hecht — *A Thousand and One Afternoons in Chicago*
Holly Iglesias — *Souvenirs of a Shrunken World*
Harriet Jacobs — *Incidents in the Life of a Slave Girl*
Paul Metcalf — *Apalache*
Maggie Nelson — *Bluets*
Kenneth Patchen — *Poemscapes*
Claudia Rankine — *Citizen: An American Lyric*
Olive Schreiner — *Dreams*
Gertrude Stein — *Tender Buttons*
William Carlos Williams — *Kora in Hell: Improvisations*

VII.
The Braided Narrative & Polyphonic Prose

Edgar Allan Poe, in "The Philosophy of Composition," asserts that "what we term a long poem is, in fact, merely a succession of brief ones— that is to say, of brief poetical effects."[31] One might also say that any long prose work—whether or not it's divided into sections—is in fact a concatenation of shorter pieces strung together.

A few years after I finished grad school, I began to write nonfiction, and I stumbled upon a form I've come to call a braided narrative. It came into the world subsequent to my falling under the spell of Harry Crosby and his cautionary tale about the illusion of true love and the tragedies to which it can lead. The short sequence, "Library," (and the longer works that followed it) consist in large part of excerpts from memoirs, letters, newspaper articles, and so forth, woven together by an observing narrative voice.[32] I originally conceived of this form as a constructed dialogue—or what one might call epistolary nonfiction. I've also seen such work referred to as *polyphonic*, as when Guy Davenport discusses the "resonating polyphony" of Paul Metcalf's writing:

> Every page of Paul Metcalf is a score for the voice. Or, as the truth is, for the imagination. For each page is a careful construct of voices, written voices for the most part, found in other texts by a searcher with eyes far sharper than ours, and infinitely more diligent in their search. [33]

This sense of the word *polyphony* goes back to its musical use, a multiplicity of voices, and the critic Irina Marchesini calls it "a new literary genre" in a recent article about Svetlana Alexievich's collection of interviews, *Chernobyl Voices*.[34] It was also used by Mikhail Bakhtin to describe the fiction of Dostoevsky:

> A genuine polyphony of fully valid voices is in fact the chief characteristic of Dostoevsky's novels. What unfolds in his works is not a multitude of characters and fates in a single objective world, illuminated by a single authorial consciousness; rather a plurality . . . combine but are not merged in the unity of the event.[35]

More recent studies in literary polyphony would include Elizabeth

Bahs' doctoral dissertation, "On the Threshold: The Polyphonic Poetry Sequence." She calls this a "genre in progress," which "has remained largely invisible in critical scholarship, yet one that many contemporary poets have chosen when working with multiple first-person perspectives."[36] Similarly, Corinne Bancroft uses the term "braided narrative" in a discussion of what she calls "a new subtype of the novel" —in which writers "plait together different narrative threads."[37]

✻   ✻   ✻

Library

> We might have given birth to a butterfly
> With the daily news
> Printed in blood on its wings
> —Mina Loy

You've been in the library now for hours. You came back after dinner and now you've fallen asleep. As a matter of fact it's so late that everyone else has left the library, but since you're tucked away in a corner by the window no one noticed you before they turned off the lights. It's April now and the moon is almost full and the clouds are scudding across the moon so it looks like the moon itself is moving quickly . . . and off to the east the lake is dark, though even if you were awake you couldn't see the lake from here, where you're sitting by the window—or more factually, slumped over with your head back and your mouth open as though you'd fallen asleep on a plane. Books, several of them, are open in front of you.

On December 10, 1929, Harry Crosby, 31, and Josephine Rotch Bigelow, 22, were found dead together in a friend's apartment. They'd been lovers for a year and a half, though each was married to someone else. The *New York Times* the next day had this to say:

> The couple had died in what Dr. Charles Morris, Medical Examiner, described as a suicide compact. The police believe that Crosby, in whose hand they found a .25 Belgian automatic pistol, had shot Mrs. Bigelow and then turned the weapon on himself. There were no notes and the authorities

were unable to obtain information pointing to a motive for the deaths.

In the dark library, in the overstuffed library chair, with the moon asserting itself through the windows your sleep is getting restless. It's almost, with the moon and the dark library, as though you're not asleep at all. It's as though you're hearing voices from far off, as if you're walking in a fog down a city street and there are people talking all around you but you can only see the glow of distant street lights and dark trees formless around you . . . and then suddenly faces appear out of the fog. This has all happened before, as a matter of fact you've been troubled with these dreams for months, but they've never been this vivid. The faces circle you, indistinct in the fog, and for the first time you can hear what they're saying. . . .

Caresse Crosby: The lazy towers of Notre Dame were framed between the curtains of our bedroom windows.

Harry Crosby: "I like my body when it is with your body. It is so quite new a thing."

Stephen Crosby: The idea of your writing poetry as a life work is a joke and makes everybody laugh.

Caresse: There was a swimming pool on the stream side of the courtyard, around whose paved shores coffee and croissants were served on summer mornings from sunrise until noon.

Harry: The shattered hull of a rowboat stuck in the sand, a fire of drift wood, a bottle of black wine, black beetles, the weird cry of sea-gulls lost in the fog, the sound of the tide creeping in over the wet sands, the tombstone in the eel-grass behind the dunes.

Hart Crane: Dinners, soirées, poets, erratic millionaires, painters, translations, lobsters, absinthe, music, promenades, oysters, sherry, asprin, pictures, Sapphic heiresses, editors, books, sailors.

Harry: What is it I want? Who is it I want to sleep with?

Josephine Rotch: Do not be depressed. Take the next boat. You know I love you and want you.

It's hard to believe you're still asleep, slouched over in the musty library chair. The moon is still poking through the clouds. If your eyes were open you'd see moonlight across the books in front of you. But you're still asleep, cramped and uncomfortable as it must be. Perhaps you'll ache tomorrow. Outside the window the trees are dark in the shadow of the library. The faces turned towards you in the fog are indistinct—a crowd of strangers who seem, unaccountably, familiar. Like the time you met her at that party, from across the room and all the noise you thought to yourself Where have I seen her before? knowing that you probably never had. And in bed the first time together, her dark eyes looking at you: Who is this woman? Yes, in the dark library, in the moonlight and the fog, you can hear the voices . . . what is it they're saying, what is it?

Archibald MacLeish: My impression was that it was all good fun, good decor, but not to be taken seriously. My own conviction was that he wasn't serious about it, till I found out the hard way that he was deadly serious about it.

Harry: When I got home a riot with Caresse and she started to jump out the window got halfway over the balcony rail. It happened so quickly that I hardly had time to be frightened but now three hours later I am really frightened I hope I don't dream about it.

Josephine: I love you I love you I love you.

Harry: It was madness, like cats in the night which howl, no longer knowing whether they are on earth or in hell or in paradise.

Josephine: Death is our marriage.

MacLeish: As I sat there looking at his corpse, seating myself where I wouldn't have to see the horrible hole in back of his ear, I kept saying to him: you poor, damned, dumb bastard.
You're awake suddenly in the dark library. The lights from Sonny's

across the street are out, it must be after four. The moon is gone. You feel like shit. Time to walk the couple of blocks home in the April darkness . . . and the birds maybe already awake. You open the library door the air's a bit chilly. There's nothing like the taste of last night's coffee, you mumble to yourself and whoever else might be listening.[38]

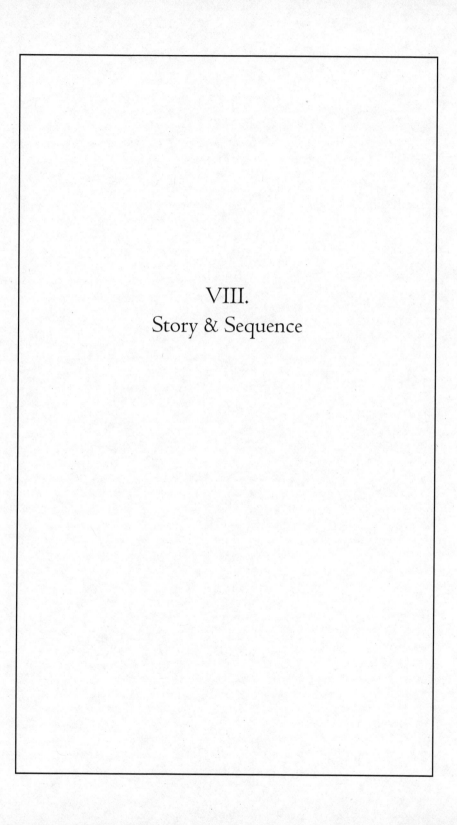

VIII.
Story & Sequence

In 1932, in the little magazine *Contact*, William Carlos Williams published a sequence of sixteen shorts titled, "For Bill Bird,"[39] Here is the first piece:

It was getting kinda late. We'd been talking cars. I wanted them to come in on a new model we had just unloaded. He seemed interested but she wouldn't let him buy it. So I kept talking, stalling along hoping for a break.

Pretty soon I hears a car pull up in front of the house and stop. I thought someone was coming in. I waited a while then I ast them if they'd heard it too.

Oh, yes, she says, that's our daughter coming home from the movies.

That was all right but after another half hour and nobody comin' in I spoke up again. I guess you were wrong, I says, about that being your daughter.

No, she says, she usually sits out there with her boyfriend for a while before coming in. I suppose she sees the light and knows we're up.

A little after twelve o'clock the car starts up and I could hear it fade out down the street. Then someone comes runnin' up the front steps. The door flings open and in comes the girl. A peach, take it from me. As soon as she sees me she stops and stands there swinging her panties around on the fingertips of her left hand.

Hello folks, she says then, and lets her underwear go onto a couch. How's everybody?

Evelyn! says her mother, I hope you're not going to bring disgrace and scandal into this house.

Oh don't worry, Mother, she says, we're careful.

The entire sequence in which this appears was later published in a somewhat different form as "World's End," in *Life Along the Passaic River* (1938). As printed there, the sequentially numbered headings are replaced by a simple space between sections. In the original publication, the numbered sections at first seem interrelated, but it's soon apparent that the pieces have in fact very little to do with each other in a narrative sense, and the reader is forced to look for correspondences among the various fragments. Seen in toto as a short story, however, this sequence has a remarkably different effect on the reader. Marjorie Perloff, for example, refers to "World's End" as "one of William Carlos Williams' autobiographical sketches about the world of the big-city hospital"—and to the speaker as a "doctor-narrator."[40]

This is just to say, of course, that presenting the narrative as a single, unified story imparts a different context to the reader's attention than when the piece is a sequence of shorts, each of which has only a numeral as its title. As a story, the narrative takes on the quality of a landscape seen from above, flattened out, only the essentials asserting themselves in the reader's vision and all else subsumed in the main pattern of rivers and fields below. But as a sequence with sixteen different moving parts, it's as though the forests and low hills grab and draw the reader down to their own level, the setting sun no longer spreading its shadows from the horizon but rather revealing through naked branches minute details of soil and forest floor, the abode of small scurrying animals. It's a different landscape altogether, though the words themselves remain the same.

✻   ✻   ✻

As the sequences grow in size the structure itself grows increasingly amorphous. I'm concluding this essay with some more examples drawn from collections I've helped edit over the past forty years. Though these sequences are, for the most part, longer than those included in my discussion of two- to five-part narratives, they are still relatively short, the longest (Hemingway's "In Our Time") having only eighteen sections, for a total of about 3,500 words. The earliest work here dates from 1887 and the most recent from 2016. Overall, these pieces are a mere bagatelle in the history of modern literature—but this reader, for one, looks forward eagerly to what future authors will bring to the form.

Emma Lazarus (1849–1887)[41]

BY THE WATERS OF THE BABYLON:
LITTLE POEMS IN PROSE

I. The Exodus (August 3, 1492)

1. The Spanish noon is a blaze of azure fire, and the dusty pilgrims crawl like an endless serpent along treeless plains and bleached high-roads, through rock-split ravines and castellated, cathedral-shadowed towns.

2. The hoary patriarch, wrinkled as an almond shell, bows painfully upon his staff. The beautiful young mother, ivory-pale, well-nigh swoons beneath her burden; in her large enfolding arms nestles her sleeping babe, round her knees flock her little ones with bruised and bleeding feet. "Mother, shall we soon be there?"

3. The youth with Christ-like countenance speaks comfortably to father and brother, to maiden and wife. In his breast, his own heart is broken.

4. The halt, the blind, are amid the train. Sturdy pack-horses laboriously drag the tented wagons wherein lie the sick athirst with fever.

5. The panting mules are urged forward with spur and goad; stuffed are the heavy saddle-bags with the wreckage of ruined homes.

6. Hark to the tinkling silver hells that adorn the tenderly-carried silken scrolls,

7. In the fierce noon glare a lad bears a kindled lamp; behind its network of bronze the airs of heaven breathe not upon its faint purple star.

8. Noble and abject, learned and simple, illustrious and obscure, plod side by side, all brothers now, all merged in one routed army of misfortune.

9. Woe to the straggler who falls by the wayside! no friend shall close his eyes.

10. They leave behind, the grape, the olive, and the fig; the vines they planted, the corn they sowed, the garden-cities of Andalusia and Aragon, Estremadura and La Mancha, of Granada and Castile; the altar, the hearth, and the grave of their fathers.

11. The townsman spits at their garments, the shepherd quits his flock, the peasant his plow, to pelt with curses and stones; the villager sets

on their trail his yelping cur.

12. Oh the weary march, oh the uptorn roots of home, oh the blankness of the receding goal!

13. Listen to their lamentation: *They that ate dainty food are desolate in the streets; they that were reared in scarlet embrace dunghills. They flee away and wander about. Men say among the nations, they shall no more sojourn there; our end is near, our days are full, our doom is come.*

14. Whither shall they turn? for the West hath cast them out, and the East refuseth to receive.

15. O bird of the air, whisper to the despairing exiles, that to-day, to-day, from the many-masted, gayly-bannered port of Palos, sails the world-unveiling Genoese, to unlock the golden gates of sunset and bequeath a Continent to Freedom!

II. Treasures

1. Through cycles of darkness the diamond sleeps in its coal-black prison.

2. Purely incrusted in its scaly casket, the breath-tarnished pear slumbers in mud and ooze.

3. Buried in tile bowels of earth, rugged and obscure, lies the ingot of gold.

4. Long hast thou been buried, O Israel, in the bowels of earth; long hast thou slumbered beneath the overwhelming waves; long hast thou slept in the rayless house of darkness.

5. Rejoice and sing, for only thus couldst thou rightly guard the golden knowledge, Truth, the delicate pearl and the adamantine jewel of the Law.

III. The Sower

1. Over a boundless plain went a man, carrying seed.

2. His face was blackened by sun and rugged from tempest, scarred and distorted by pain. Naked to the loins, his back was ridged with furrows, his breast was plowed with stripes.

3. From his hand dropped the fecund seed.

4. And behold, instantly started from the prepared soil a blade, a

sheaf, a springing trunk, a myriad-branching, cloud-aspiring tree. Its arms touched the ends of the horizon, the heavens were darkened with its shadow.

5. It bare blossoms of gold and blossoms of blood, fruitage of health and fruitage of poison; birds sang amid its foliage, and a serpent was coiled about its stem.

6. Under its branches a divinely beautiful man, crowned with thorns, was nailed to a cross.

7. And the tree put forth treacherous boughs to strangle the Sower; his flesh was bruised and torn, but cunningly he disentangled the murderous knot and passed to the eastward.

8. Again there dropped from his hand the fecund seed.

9. And behold, instantly started from the prepared soil a blade, a sheaf, a springing trunk, a myriad-branching, cloud-aspiring tree. Crescent-shaped like little emerald moons were the leaves; it bare blossoms of silver and blossoms of blood, fruitage of health and fruitage of poison; birds sang amid its foliage and a serpent was coiled about its stem.

10. Under its branches a turbaned mighty-limbed Prophet brandished a drawn sword.

11. And behold, this tree likewise puts forth perfidious arms to strangle the Sower; but cunningly he disentangles the murderous knot and passes on.

12. Lo, his hands are not empty of grain, the strength of his arm is not spent.

13. What germ hast thou saved for the future, O miraculous Husbandman? Tell me, thou Planter of Christhood and Islam; tell me, thou seedbearing Israel!

IV. The Test

1. Daylong I brooded upon the Passion of Israel.

2. I saw him bound to the wheel, nailed to the cross, cut off by the sword, burned at the stake, tossed into the seas.

3. And always the patient, resolute, martyr face arose in silent rebuke and defiance.

4. A Prophet with four eyes; wide gazed the orbs of the spirit above the sleeping eyelids of the senses.

5. A Poet, who plucked from his bosom the quivering heart and

fashioned it into a lyre.

6. A placid-browed Sage, uplifted from earth in celestial meditation.

7. These I saw, with princes and people in their train; the monumental dead and the standard-bearers of the future.

8. And suddenly I heard a burst of mocking laughter, and turning, I beheld the shuffling gait, the ignominious features, the sordid mask of the son of the Ghetto.

V. Currents

1. Vast oceanic movements, the flux and reflux of immeasurable tides oversweep our continent.

2. From the far Caucasian steppes, from the squalid Ghettos of Europe,

3. From Odessa and Bucharest, from Kief and Ekaterinoslav,

4. Hark to the cry of the exiles of Babylon, the voice of Rachel mourning for her children, of Israel lamenting for Zion.

5. And lo, like a turbid stream, the long-pent flood bursts the dykes of oppression and rushes hitherward.

6. Unto her ample breast, the generous mother of nations welcomes them.

7. The herdsman of Canaan and the seed of Jerusalem's royal shepherd renew their youth amid the pastoral plains of Texas and the golden valleys of the Sierras.

VI. The Prophet

1. Moses ben Maimon lifting his perpetual lamp over the path of the perplexed;

2. Hallevi, the honey-tongued poet, wakening amid the silent ruins of Zion the sleeping lyre of David;

3. Moses, the wise son of Mendel, who made the Ghetto illustrious;

4. Abarbanel, the counselor of kings; Alcharisi, the exquisite singer; Ibn Ezra, the perfect old man; Gabirol, the tragic seer;

5. Heine, the enchanted magician, the heart-broken jester;

6. Yea, and the century-crowned patriarch whose bounty engirdles the globe;—

7. These need no wreath and no trumpet; like perennial asphodel blossoms, their fame, their glory resounds like the brazen-throated comet.

8. But thou—hast thou faith in the fortune of Israel? Wouldst thou lighten the anguish of Jacob?

9. Then shalt thou take the hand of yonder caftaned wretch with flowing curls and gold-pierced ears;

10. Who crawls blinking forth from the loathsome recesses of the Jewry;

11. Nerveless his fingers, puny his frame; haunted by the bat-like phantoms of superstition is his brain.

12. Thou shalt say to the bigot, "My Brother," and to the creature of darkness, "My Friend."

13. And thy heart shall spend itself in fountains of love upon the ignorant, the coarse, and the abject.

14. Then in the obscurity thou shalt hear a rush of wings, thine eyes shall be bitten with pungent smoke.

15. And close against thy quivering lips shall be pressed the live coal wherewith the Seraphim brand the Prophets,

VII. Chrysalis

1. Long, long has the Orient-Jew spun around his helplessness the cunningly enmeshed web of Talmud and Kabbala.

2. Imprisoned in dark corners of misery and oppression, closely he drew about him the dust-gray filaments, soft as silk and stubborn as steel, until he lay death-stiffened in mummied seclusion.

3. And the world has named him an ugly worm, shunning the blessed daylight.

4. But when the emancipating springtide breathes wholesome, quickening airs, when the Sun of Love shines out with cordial fires, lo, the Soul of Israel bursts her cobweb sheath, and flies forth attired in the winged beauty of immortality.

Edith Wharton (1862–1937)[42]

THE VALLEY OF CHILDISH THINGS
AND OTHER EMBLEMS

I.

Once upon a time a number of children lived together in the Valley of Childish Things, playing all manner of delightful games, and studying the same lesson-books. But one day a little girl, one of their number, decided that it was time to see something of the world about which the lesson-books had taught her; and as none of the other children cared to leave their games, she set out alone to climb the pass which led out of the valley.

It was a hard climb, but at length she reached a cold, bleak table-land beyond the mountains. Here she saw cities and men, and learned many useful arts, and in so doing grew to be a woman. But the table-land was bleak and cold, and when she had served her apprenticeship she decided to return to her old companions in the Valley of Childish Things, and work with them instead of with strangers.

It was a weary way back, and her feet were bruised by the stones, and her face was beaten by the weather; but half way down the pass she met a man, who kindly helped her over the roughest places. Like herself, he was lame and weather-beaten; but as soon as he spoke she recognized him as one of her old play-mates. He too had been out in the world, and was going back to the valley; and on the way they talked together of the work they meant to do there. He had been a dull boy, and she had never taken much notice of him; but as she listened to his plans for building bridges and draining swamps and cutting roads through the jungle, she thought to herself, "Since he has grown into such a fine fellow, what splendid men and women my other playmates must have become!"

But what was her surprise to find, on reaching the valley, that her former companions, instead of growing into men and women, had all remained little children. Most of them were playing the same old games, and the few who affected to be working were engaged in such strenuous occupations as building mudpies and sailing paper boats in basins. As for the lad who had been the favorite companion of her studies, he was playing marbles with all the youngest boys in the valley.

At first the children seemed glad to have her back, but soon she saw that her presence interfered with their games; and when she tried to tell them of the great things that were being done on the table-land beyond the mountains, they picked up their toys and went farther down the valley to play.

Then she turned to her fellow-traveler, who was the only grown man in the valley; but he was on his knees before a dear little girl with blue eyes and a coral necklace, for whom he was making a garden out of cockle-shells and bits of glass, and broken flowers stuck in sand.

The little girl was clapping her hands and crowing (she was too young to speak articulately); and when she who had grown to be a woman laid her hand on the man's shoulder, and asked him if he did not want to set to work with her building bridges, draining swamps, and cutting roads through the jungle, he replied that at that particular moment he was too busy.

And as she turned away, he added in the kindest possible way, "Really, my dear, you ought to have taken better care of your complexion."

II.

There was once a maiden lady who lived alone in a commodious brick house facing north and south. The lady was very fond of warmth and sunshine, but unfortunately her room was on the north side of the house, so that in winter she had no sun at all.

This distressed her so much that, after long deliberation, she sent for an architect, and asked him if it would be possible to turn the house around so that her room should face the south. The architect replied that anything could be done for money, but the estimated cost of turning the house around was so high that the lady, who enjoyed a handsome income, was obliged to reduce her way of living and sell her securities at a sacrifice to raise money enough for the purpose.

At length, however, the house was turned around, and she felt almost consoled for her impoverishment by the first ray of sunlight which stole through her shutters the next morning.

That very day she received a visit from an old friend who had been absent a year; and this friend, finding her seated at her window in a flood of sunlight, immediately exclaimed:

"My dear, how sensible of you to have moved into a south room! I never could understand why you persisted so long in living on the north side of the house."

And the following day the architect sent in his bill.

III.

There was once a little girl who was so very intelligent that her parents feared that she would die.

But an aged aunt, who had crossed the Atlantic in a sailing-vessel, said, "My dears, let her marry the first man she falls in love with, and she will make such a fool of herself that it will probably save her life."

IV.

A thinly clad man, who was trudging afoot through a wintry and shelterless region, met another wrapped in a big black cloak. The cloak hung heavily on its wearer, and seemed to drag him back, but at least it kept off the cold.

"That's a fine warm cloak you've got" said the first man through his chattering teeth.

"Oh," said the other, "it's none of my choosing, I promise you. It's only my old happiness dyed black and made over into a sorrow; but in this weather a man must wear what he's got."

"To think of some people's luck!" muttered the first man, as the other passed on. "Now I never had enough happiness to make a sorrow out of."

V.

There was once a man who married a sweet little wife; but when he set out with her from her father's house, he found that she had never been taught to walk. They had a long way to go, and there was nothing for him to do but to carry her; and as he carried her she grew heavier and heavier.

Then they came to a wide, deep river, and he found that she had never been taught to swim. So he told her to hold fast to his shoulder, and started to swim with her across the river. And as he swam she grew frightened, and dragged him down in her struggles. And the river was deep and wide, and the current ran fast; and once or twice she nearly had him under. But he fought his way through, and landed her safely on the other side; and behold, he found himself in a strange country, beyond all imagining delightful. And as he looked about him and gave thanks, he said to himself:

"Perhaps if I hadn't had to carry her over, I shouldn't have kept up long enough to get here myself."

VI.

A soul once cowered in a gray waste, and a mighty shape came by. Then the soul cried out for help, saying, "Shall I be left to perish alone in this desert of Unsatisfied Desires?"

"But you are mistaken," the shape replied; "this is the land of Gratified Longings. And, moreover, you are not alone, for the country is full of people; but whoever tarries here grows blind."

VII.

There was once a very successful architect who made a great name for himself. At length he built a magnificent temple, to which he devoted more time and thought than to any of the other buildings he had erected; and the world pronounced it his masterpiece. Shortly afterward he died, and when he came before the judgment angel he was not asked how many sins he had committed, but how many houses he had built.

He hung his head and said, more than he could count.

The judgment angel asked what they were like, and the architect said that he was afraid they were pretty bad.

"And are you sorry?" asked the angel.

"Very sorry," said the architect, with honest contrition.

"And how about that famous temple that you built just before you died?" the angel continued. "Are you satisfied with that?"

"Oh, no," the architect exclaimed. "I really think it has some good points about it,—I did try my best, you know,—but there's one dreadful mistake that I'd give my soul to go back and rectify."

"Well," said the angel, "you can't go back and rectify it, but you can take your choice of the following alternatives: either we can let the world go on thinking your temple a masterpiece and you the greatest architect that ever lived, or we can send to earth a young fellow we've got here who will discover your mistake at a glance, and point it out so clearly to posterity that you'll be the laughing-stock of all succeeding generations of architects. Which do you choose?"

"Oh, well," said the architect, "if it comes to that, you know—as long as it suits my clients as it is, I really don't see the use of making such a fuss."

VIII.

A man once married a charming young person who agreed with him on every question. At first they were very happy, for the man thought his wife the most interesting companion he had ever met, and they spent their days telling each other what wonderful people they were. But by and by the man began to find his wife rather tiresome. Wherever he went she insisted upon going; whatever he did, she was sure to tell him that it would have been better to do the opposite; and moreover, it gradually dawned upon him that his friends had never thought so highly of her as he did. Having made this discovery, he naturally felt justified in regarding himself as the aggrieved party; she took the same view of her situation, and their life was one of incessant recrimination.

Finally, after years spent in violent quarrels and short-lived reconciliations, the man grew weary, and decided to divorce his wife.

He engaged an able lawyer, who assured him that he would have no difficulty in obtaining a divorce; but to his surprise, the judge refused to grant it.

"But—" said the man, and he began to recapitulate his injuries.

"That's all very true," said the judge, "and nothing would be easier than for you to obtain a divorce if you had only married another person."

"What do you mean by another person?" asked the man in astonishment.

"Well," replied the judge, "it appears that you inadvertently married yourself; that is a union no court has the power to dissolve."

"Oh," said the man; and he was secretly glad, for in his heart he was already longing to make it up again with his wife.

IX.

There was once a gentleman who greatly disliked to assume any re-
sponsibility. Being possessed of ample means and numerous poor relatives,
he might have indulged a variety of tastes and even a few virtues; but since
there is no occupation that does not bring a few cares in its train, this gen-
tleman resolutely refrained from doing anything.

He ceased to visit his old mother, who lived in the country, because
it made him nervous to catch the train; he subscribed to no charities because
it was a bother to write the checks; he received no visits because he did not
wish to be under the obligation of returning them; he invited no guests to
stay with him, for fear of being bored before they left; he gave no presents
because it was so troublesome to choose them; finally, be even gave up asking
his friends to dine because it was such a nuisance to tell the cook that they
were coming.

This gentleman took an honest pride in his complete detachment
from the trivial importunities of life, and was never tired of ridiculing those
who complained of the weight of their responsibilities, justly remarking that
if they really wished to be their own masters they had only to follow his ex-
ample.

One day, however, one of his servants carelessly left the front door
open, and Death walked in unannounced, and begged the gentleman to come
along as quickly as possible, as there were a good many more people to be
called for that afternoon.

"But I can't," cried the gentleman, in dismay. "I really can't, you know.
I—why, I've asked some people to dine with me this evening."

"That's a little too much," said Death. And the devil carried the gen-
tleman off in a big black bag.

X.

There was once a man who had seen the Parthenon, and he wished
to build his god a temple like it.

But he was not a skillful man, and, try as be would, he could produce
only a mud hut thatched with straw; and he sat down and wept because he
could not build a temple for his god.

But one who passed by said to him:

"There are two worse plights than yours. One is to have no god; the other is to build a mud hut and mistake it for the Parthenon."

Fenton Johnson (1888–1958)[43]

AFRICAN NIGHTS

Tired

I am tired of work; I am tired of building up somebody else's civilization.

Let us take a rest, M'Lissy Jane.

I will go down to the Last Chance Saloon, drink a gallon or two of gin, shoot a game or two of dice and sleep the rest of the night on one of Mike's barrels.

You will let the old shanty go to rot, the white people's clothes turn to dust, and the Calvary Baptist Church sink to the bottom-less pit.

You will spend your days forgetting you married me and your nights hunting the warm gin Mike serves the ladies in the rear of the Last Chance Saloon.

Throw the children into the river; civilization has given us too many. It is better to die than it is to grow up and find out that you are colored.

Pluck the stars out of the heavens. The stars mark our destiny. The stars marked my destiny.

I am tired of civilization.

Aunt Hannah Jackson

Despite her sixty years Aunt Hannah Jackson rubs on other people's clothes.

Time has played havoc with her eyes and turned to gray her parched hair.

But her tongue is nimble as she talks to herself.

All day she talks to herself about her neighbors and her friends and the man she loved.

Yes, Aunt Hannah Jackson loved even as you and I and Wun Hop Sing.

"He was a good man," she says, "but a fool."

"So am I a fool and Mrs. Lee a fool and this Mrs. Goldstein that I work for a fool."

All of us are fools."

For rubbing on other people's clothes Aunt Hannah Jackson gets a dollar and fifty cents a day and a worn out dress on Christmas.

For talking to herself Aunt Hannah Jackson gets a smile as we call her a good natured fool.

Aunt Jane Allen

State Street is lonely today. Aunt Jane Allen has driven her chariot to Heaven.

I remember how she hobbled along, a little woman, parched of skin, brown as the leather of a satchel and with eyes that had scanned eighty years of life.

Have those who bore her dust to the last resting place buried with her the basket of aprons she went up and down State Street trying to sell?

Have those who bore her dust to the last resting place buried with her the gentle word Son that she gave to each of the seed of Ethiopia?

The Barber

I wield the razor, sling hot towels and talk.

My daily newspaper is the racing chart and my pastime making bets on fleet-footed horses.

Whatever is left from betting I divide with my wife and a yellow woman who lives in an apartment on Wabash Avenue.

(Poor Wife! She gets very little.)

I love gay clothes, a good supply of Fatimas and the fire in gin and whiskey.

I love life. Who doesn't?

The Drunkard

I had a wife, but she is gone. She left me a week ago. God bless her!

I married another in the rear of Mike's saloon. It was a gallon jug of the reddest liquor that ever burned the throat of man. I will be true to my new wife. You can have the other.

The Banjo Player

There is music in me, the music of a peasant people.

I wander through the levee, picking my banjo and singing my songs of the cabin and the field. At the Last Chance Saloon I am as welcome as the violets in March; there is always food and drink for me there, and the dimes of those who love honest music. Behind the railroad tracks the little children clap their hands and love me as they love Kris Kringle.

But I fear that I am a failure. Last night a woman called me a troubadour. What is a troubadour?

The Minister

I mastered pastoral theology, the Greek of the Apostles, and all the difficult subjects in a minister's curriculum.

I was as learned as any in this country when the Bishop ordained me.

And I went to preside over Mount Moriah, largest flock in the Conference.

I preached the Word as I felt it, I visited the sick and dying and comforted the afflicted in spirit.

I loved my work because I loved my God.

But I lost my charge to Sam Jenkins, who has not been to school four years in his life.

I lost my charge because I could not make my congregation shout.

And my dollar money was small, very small.

Sam Jenkins can tear a Bible to tatters and his congregation destroys the pews with their shouting and stamping.

Sam Jenkins leads in the gift of raising dollar money.
Such is religion.

The Scarlet Woman

Once I was good like the Virgin Mary and the Minister's wife.

My father worked for Mr. Pullman and white people's tips; but he died two days after his insurance expired.

I had nothing, so I had to go to work.

All the stock I had was a white girl's education and a face that enchanted the men of both races.

Starvation danced with me.

So when Big Lizzie, who kept a house for white men, came to me with tales of fortune that I could reap from the sale of my virtue I bowed my head to Vice.

Now I can drink more gin than any man for miles around.

Gin is better than all the water in Lethe.

Ernest Hemingway (1899–1961)[44]

IN OUR TIME

Chapter 1

Everybody was drunk. The whole battery was drunk going along the road in the dark. We were going to the Champagne. The lieutenant kept riding his horse out into the fields and saying to him, "I'm drunk, I tell you, mon vieux. Oh, I am so soused." We went along the road all night in the dark and the adjutant kept riding up alongside my kitchen and saying, "You must put it out. It is dangerous. It will be observed." We were fifty kilometers from the front but the adjutant worried about the fire in my kitchen. It was funny going along that road. That was when I was a kitchen corporal.

Chapter 2

The first matador got the horn through his sword hand and the crowd hooted him out. The second matador slipped and the bull caught him through the belly and he hung on to the horn with one hand and held the other tight against the place, and the bull rammed him wham against the wall and the horn came out, and he lay in the sand, and then got up like crazy drunk and tried to slug the men carrying him away and yelled for his sword but he fainted. The kid came out and had to kill five bulls because you can't have more than three matadors, and the last bull he was so tired he couldn't get the sword in. He couldn't hardly lift his arm. He tried five times and the crowd was quiet because it was a good bull and it looked like him or the bull and then he finally made it. He sat down in the sand and puked and they held a cape over him while the crowd hollered and threw things down into the bull ring.

Chapter 3

Minarets stuck up in the rain out of Adrianople across the mud flats. The carts were jammed for thirty miles along the Karagatch road. Water buffalo and cattle were hauling carts through the mud. No end and no beginning. Just carts loaded with everything they owned. The old men and women, soaked through, walked along keeping the cattle moving. The Maritza was running yellow almost up to the bridge. Carts were jammed solid on the bridge with camels bobbing along through them. Greek cavalry herded along the procession. Women and kids were in the carts crouched with mattresses, mirrors, sewing machines, bundles. There was a woman having a kid with a young girl holding a blanket over her and crying. Scared sick looking at it. It rained all through the evacuation.

Chapter 4

We were in a garden at Mons. Young Buckley came in with his patrol from across the river. The first German I saw climbed up over the garden wall. We waited till he got one leg over and then potted him. He had so much equipment on and looked awfully surprised and fell down into the garden. Then three more came over further down the wall. We shot them. They all came just like that.

Chapter 5

It was a frightfully hot day. We'd jammed an absolutely perfect barricade across the bridge. It was simply priceless. A big old wrought iron grating from the front of a house. Too heavy to lift and you could shoot through it and they would have to climb over it. It was absolutely topping. They tried to get over it, and we potted them from forty yards. They rushed it, and officers came out alone and worked on it. It was an absolutely perfect obstacle. Their officers were very fine. We were frightfully put out when we heard the flank had gone, and we had to fall back.

Chapter 6

They shot the six cabinet ministers at half-past six in the morning against the wall of a hospital. There were pools of water in the courtyard. There were wet dead leaves on the paving of the courtyard. It rained hard. All the shutters of the hospital were nailed shut. One of the ministers was sick with typhoid. Two soldiers carried him downstairs and out into the rain. They tried to hold him up against the wall but he sat down in a puddle of water.

The other five stood very quietly against the wall. Finally the officer told the soldiers it was no good trying to make him stand up. When they fired the first volley he was sitting down in the water with his head on his knees.

Chapter 7

Nick sat against the wall of the church where they had dragged him to be clear of machine gun fire in the street. Both legs stuck out awkwardly. He had been hit in the spine. His face was sweaty and dirty. The sun shone on his face. The day was very hot. Rinaldi, big backed, his equipment sprawling, lay face downward against the wall. Nick looked straight ahead brilliantly. The pink wall of the house opposite had fallen out from the roof, and an iron bedstead hung twisted toward the street. Two Austrian dead lay in the rubble in the shade of the house. Up the street were other dead. Things were getting forward in the town. It was going well. Stretcher bearers would be along any time now. Nick turned his head carefully and looked down at Rinaldi. "Senta Rinaldi. Senta. You and me we've made a separate peace." Rinaldi lay still in the sun breathing with difficulty. "Not patriots." Nick turned his head carefully away smiling sweatily. Rinaldi was a disappointing audience.

Chapter 8

While the bombardment was knocking the trench to pieces at Fossalta, he lay very flat and sweated and prayed oh jesus christ get me out of here. Dear jesus please get me out. Christ please please please christ. If you'll only keep me from getting killed I'll do anything you say. I believe in you and I'll tell everyone in the world that you are the only thing that matters. Please please dear jesus. The shelling moved further up the line. We went to work on the trench and in the morning the sun came up and the day was hot and muggy and cheerful and quiet. The next night back at Mestre he did not tell the girl he went upstairs with at the Villa Rossa about Jesus. And he never told anybody.

Chapter 9

At two o'clock in the morning two Hungarians got into a cigar store at Fifteenth Street and Grand Avenue. Drevitts and Boyle drove up from the

Fifteenth Street police station in a Ford. The Hungarians were backing their wagon out of an alley. Boyle shot one off the seat of the wagon and one out of the wagon box. Drevitts got frightened when he found they were both dead. Hell Jimmy, he said, you oughtn't to have done it. There's liable to be a hell of a lot of trouble.

—They're crooks ain't they? said Boyle. They're wops ain't they? Who the hell is going to make any trouble?

—That's all right maybe this time, said Drevitts, but how did you know they were wops when you bumped them?

Wops, said Boyle, I can tell wops a mile off.

Chapter 10

One hot evening in Milan they carried him up onto the roof and he could look out over the top of the town. There were chimney swifts in the sky. After a while it got dark and the searchlights came out. The others went down and took the bottles with them. He and Ag could hear them below on the balcony. Ag sat on the bed. She was cool and fresh in the hot night.

Ag stayed on night duty for three months. They were glad to let her. When they operated on him she prepared him for the operating table, and they had a joke about friend or enema. He went under the anesthetic holding tight on to himself so that he would not blab about anything during the silly, talky time. After he got on crutches he used to take the temperature so Ag would not have to get up from the bed. There were only a few patients, and they all knew about it. They all liked Ag. As he walked back along the halls he thought of Ag in his bed.

Before he went back to the front they went into the Duomo and prayed. It was dim and quiet, and there were other people praying. They wanted to get married, but there was not enough time for the banns, and neither of them had birth certificates. They felt as though they were married, but they wanted everyone to know about it, and to make it so they could not lose it.

Ag wrote him many letters that he never got until after the armistice. Fifteen came in a bunch and he sorted them by the dates and read them all straight through. They were about the hospital, and how much she loved him and how it was impossible to get along without him and how terrible it was missing him at night.

After the armistice they agreed he should go home to get a job so they might be married. Ag would not come home until he had a good job and could come to New York to meet her. It was understood he would not drink, and he did not want to see his friends or anyone in the States. Only to get a job and be married. On the train from Padova to Milan they quarreled about her not being willing to come home at once. When they had to say good-bye in the station at Padova they kissed good-bye, but were not finished with the quarrel. He felt sick about saying good-bye like that.

He went to America on a boat from Genoa. Ag went back to Torre di Mosta to open a hospital. It was lonely and rainy there, and there was a battalion of arditi quartered in the town. Living in the muddy, rainy town in the winter the major of the battalion made love to Ag, and she had never known Italians before, and finally wrote a letter to the States that theirs had been only a boy and girl affair. She was sorry, and she knew he would probably not be able to understand, but might some day forgive her, and be grateful to her, and she expected, absolutely unexpectedly, to be married in the spring. She loved him as always, but she realized now it was only a boy and girl love. She hoped he would have a great career, and believed in him absolutely. She knew it was for the best.

The Major did not marry her in the spring, or any other time. Ag never got an answer to her letter to Chicago about it. A short time after he contracted gonorrhea from a sales girl from The Fair riding in a taxicab through Lincoln Park.

Chapter 11

In 1919 he was travelling on the railroads in Italy carrying a square of oilcloth from the headquarters of the party written in indelible pencil and saying here was a comrade who had suffered very much under the whites in Budapest and requesting comrades to aid him in any way. He used this instead of a ticket. He was very shy and quite young and the train men passed him on from one crew to another. He had no money, and they fed him behind the counter in railway eating houses.

He was delighted with Italy. It was a beautiful country he said. The people were all kind. He had been in many towns, walked much and seen many pictures. Giotto, Masaccio, and Piero della Francesca he bought reproductions of and carried them wrapped in a copy of Avanti. Mantegna he did not like.

He reported at Bologna, and I took him with me up into the Romagna where it was necessary I go to see a man. We had a good trip together. It was early September and the country was pleasant. He was a Magyar, a very nice boy and very shy. Horthy's men had done some bad things to him. He talked about it a little. In spite of Italy, he believed altogether in the world revolution.

—But how is the movement going in Italy? he asked.

—Very badly, I said.

—But it will go better, he said. You have everything here. It is the one country that everyone is sure of. It will be the starting point of everything.

At Bologna he said good-bye to us to go on the train to Milano and then to Aosta to walk over the pass into Switzerland. I spoke to him about the Mantegnas in Milano. No, he said, very shyly, he did not like Mantegna. I wrote out for him where to eat in Milano and the addresses of comrades. He thanked me very much, but his mind was already looking forward to walking over the pass. He was very eager to walk over the pass while the weather held good. The last I heard of him the Swiss had him in jail near Sion.

Chapter 12

They whack whacked the white horse on the legs and he knee-ed himself up. The picador twisted the stirrups straight and pulled and hauled up into the saddle. The horse's entrails hung down in a blue bunch and swung backward and forward as he began to canter, the *monos* whacking him on the back of his legs with the rods. He cantered jerkily along the barrera. He stopped stiff and one of the monos held his bridle and walked him forward. The picador kicked in his spurs, leaned forward and shook his lance at the bull. Blood pumped regularly from between the horse's front legs. He was nervously wobbly. The bull could not make up his mind to charge.

Chapter 13

The crowd shouted all the time and threw pieces of bread down into the ring, then cushions and leather wine bottles, keeping up whistling and yelling. Finally the bull was too tired from so much bad sticking and folded his knees and lay down and one of the *cuadrilla* leaned out over his neck and killed him with the *puntillo*. The crowd came over the barrera and around the torero and two men grabbed him and held him and some one cut off his pigtail and was waving it and a kid grabbed it and ran away with it. Afterwards I saw him at the café. He was very short with a brown face and quite drunk and he said after all it has happened before like that. I am not really a good bull fighter.

Chapter 14

If it happened right down close in front of you, you could see Villalta snarl at the bull and curse him, and when the bull charged he swung back firmly like an oak when the wind hits it, his legs tight together, the muleta trailing and the sword following the curve behind. Then he cursed the bull, flopped the muleta at him, and swung back from the charge his feet firm, the muleta curving and each swing the crowd roaring.

When he started to kill it was all in the same rush. The bull looking at him straight in front, hating. He drew out the sword from the folds of the muleta and sighted with the same movement and called to the bull, Toro! Toro! and the bull charged and Villalta charged and just for a moment they became one. Villalta became one with the bull and then it was over. Villalta standing straight and the red kilt of the sword sticking out dully between the bull's shoulders. Villalta, his hand up at the crowd and the bull roaring blood, looking straight at Villalta and his legs caving.

Chapter 15

I heard the drums coming down the street and then the fifes and the pipes and then they came around the corner, all dancing. The street full of them. Maera saw him and then I saw him. When they stopped the music for the crouch he hunched down in the street with them all and when they started it again he jumped up and went dancing down the street with them. He was drunk all right.

You go down after him, said Maera, he hates me.

So I went down and caught up with them and grabbed him while he was crouched down waiting for the music to break loose and said, Come on Luis. For Christ sake you've got bulls this afternoon. He didn't listen to me, he was listening so hard for the music to start.

I said, Don't be a damn fool Luis. Come on back to the hotel.

Then the music started up again and he jumped up and twisted away from me and started dancing. I grabbed his arm and he pulled loose and said, Oh leave me alone. You're not my father.

I went back to the hotel and Maera was on the balcony looking out to see if I'd be bringing him back. He went inside when he saw me and came downstairs disgusted.

Well, I said, after all he's just an ignorant Mexican savage.

Yes, Maera said, and who will kill his bulls after he gets a cogida?

We, I suppose, I said.

Yes, we, said Maera. We kills the savages' bulls, and the drunkards' bulls, and the riau-riau dancers' bulls. Yes. We kill them. We kill them all right. Yes. Yes. Yes.

Chapter 16

Maera lay still, his head on his arms, his face in the sand. He felt warm and sticky from the bleeding. Each time he felt the horn coming. Sometimes the bull only bumped him with his head. Once the horn went all the way through him and he felt it go into the sand. Someone had the bull by the tail. They were swearing at him and flopping the cape in his face. Then the bull was gone. Some men picked Maera up and started to run with him toward the barriers through the gate out the passage way around under the grand stand to the infirmary. They laid Maera down on a cot and one of the men went out for the doctor. The others stood around. The doctor came running from the corral where he had been sewing up picador horses. He had to stop and wash his hands. There was a great shouting going on in the grandstand overhead. Maera wanted to say something and found he could not talk. Maera felt everything getting larger and larger and then smaller and smaller. Then it got larger and larger and larger and then smaller and smaller. Then everything commenced to run faster and faster as when they speed up a cinematograph film. Then he was dead.

Chapter 17

They hanged Sam Cardinella at six o'clock in the morning in the corridor of the county jail. The corridor was high and narrow with tiers of cells on either side. All the cells were occupied. The men had been brought in for the hanging. Five men sentenced to be hanged were in the five top cells. Three of the men to be hanged were negroes. They were very frightened. One of the white men sat on his cot with his head in his hands. The other lay flat on his cot with a blanket wrapped around his head.

They came out onto the gallows through a door in the wall. There were six or seven of them including two priests. They were carrying Sam Cardinella. He had been like that since about four o'clock in the morning.

While they were strapping his legs together two guards held him up and the two priests were whispering to him. "Be a man, my son," said one priest. When they came toward him with the cap to go over his head Sam Cardinella lost control of his sphincter muscle. The guards who had been holding him up dropped him. They were both disgusted. "How about a chair, Will?" asked one of the guards, "Better get one," said a man in a derby hat.

When they all stepped back on the scaffolding back of the drop, which was very heavy, built of oak and steel and swung on ball bearings, Sam Cardinella was left sitting there strapped tight, the younger of the two priests kneeling beside the chair. The priest skipped back onto the scaffolding just before the drop fell.

Chapter 18

The king was working in the garden. He seemed very glad to see me. We walked through the garden. This is the queen, he said. She was clipping a rose bush. Oh how do you do, she said. We sat down at a table under a big tree and the king ordered whiskey and soda. We have good whiskey anyway, he said. The revolutionary committee, he told me, would not allow him to go outside the palace grounds. Plastiras is a very good man I believe, he said, but frightfully difficult. I think he did right though shooting those chaps. If Kerensky had shot a few men things might have been altogether different. Of course the great thing in this sort of an affair is not to be shot oneself!

It was very jolly. We talked for a long time. Like all Greeks he wanted to go to America.

Kay Boyle (1902–1992)[45]

SUMMER

I

Flying curved to the wind shearwaters turn their bodies in the wave. Sea hisses under the weed-hair, ice-armored foam plucked to vermillion bubbles by the beak of the wind. Rocks crouch under the gold hill where cypresses groove darkly like a negro lying down in wheat.

II

I press through the enclosing darkness to the window. Sky is torn sharp as steel on the yucca horns, clouds pierced tight as whorls on the yucca horns, plaques of firm flame-black on black embracing darkness that curve up to sleek and handsome yucca horns. Hysteria of the trees is palpable through the closed window and the wall. The dry tongue of my sheet turns me slowly, tentatively.

III

Wind, tendinous, drifting dark and subtle in the channel, indolent, with one arm stroking the shore. Reeds follow the movement, flowing to light, following the mystery of muscles liberated under flesh.

Wind, fingering the rain and the melon-flowers. . . the black-horned fungus growing under rye.

IV

August crops wrinkled with young cabbages deplanted and wilting in the new soil. Weight of the deflated flesh, the white-corded bel- lies, topples the spindle-stems. Blood, still as a snail's track, bulges the blue veins. There is an obscene chastity in the white potted skin. The white peak of the leaf presses the dark soil, rearing the white body upward.

V LABOR HORSES

Stones draw sharp threads of blood across your hoofs. Whips pry upon your hooded silence, men's voices shrill at the unshaken core.

The young mare passing, preens her petaled throat, thin nostrils cupping quivering globes of flame. Tongues lolling below sagged withers, fumble an old response. No glittering coil, drawn like a miracle, unfurls no strong sweet rings of flame. The empty-caverned loins open parched mouths, gape wearily away. . .

Your eyes are wounds, your bones old weapons rotting in the flesh.

VI BEFORE STORM

Firm palm of the sky curved above the roofs and the sharp river; dark unshaken palm above the yellow fire of mustard-weed and the savage sunflowers pacing across the dust. The palm is closed. The fields twist in their scarlet ribs, the valleys quiver in shadow, the wagonroads flutter like white ribbons from the proud dark wrist. . . the palm curved dark and imminent, unopened . . .

VII MONASTERY

Petalless vines of light stain the window with tendrils. Walls stretch their bleached dark—fibred limbs across the hill.

On the blue lake in his hair, his palms, white-throated, fold their wings and linger. Evening shuffles in as he walks, breaking radiant foliage on the sunset, bearing great bunches of rich black and seedless grape.

VIII WHORE STREET

Street bruised blue from the nudge of the wind, artery clogged with the setting sun. A white curtain trembles like a blade undrawn from the quick. Bed, baring firm iron limbs, scars the approach of darkness.

Breasts swing in slow delirious rhythm, caressing the odors that twitch unslaked in the gutter. Eyes press upon the withered mandarin of sun.

The night resmoothes his hair . . . memory dangling hot tongues . . . behind his eyes the white ripe fruit, the wine that crouches at the core . . . a white arm lifted, odor from the pit staining the sagging mattress of the sea.

Donald Hall (1928–2018)[46]

FLIES

—for Kate Wells, 1878–1975

A fly sleeps on the field of a green curtain. I sit by my grandmother's side, and rub her head as if I could comfort her. Ninety-seven years. Her eyes stay closed, her mouth open, and she gasps in her blue nightgown—pale blue, washed a thousand times. Now her face goes white, and her breath slows until I think it has stopped; then she gasps again, and pink returns to her face.

Between the roof of her month and her tongue, strands of spittle waver as she breathes. Now a nurse shakes her head over my grandmother's sore mouth, and goes to get a glass of water, a spoon, and a flyswatter. My grandmother chokes on a spoonful of water and the nurse swats the fly.

*　*　*

In the Connecticut suburbs where I grew up, and in Ann Arbor, there were houses with small leaded panes, where Formica shone in the kitchens, and hardwood in closets under paired leather boots. Carpets lay thick underfoot in every bedroom, bright, clean, with no dust or hair in them. Nothing looked used, in these houses. Forty dollars' worth of cut flowers leaned from Waterford vases for the Saturday dinner party.

Even in houses like these, the housefly wandered and paused—and I listened for the *buzz* of its wings and its tiny feet, as it struggled among cut flowers and bumped into leaded panes.

*　*　*

In the afternoon my mother takes over at my grandmother's side in the Peabody Home, while I go back to the farm. I nap in the room my mother and my grandmother were born in.

At night we assemble beside her. Her shallow, rapid breath rasps, and her eyes jerk. and the nurse can find no pulse, as her small strength concentrates wholly on half an inch of lung space, and she coughs faintly—quick coughs like fingertips on a ledge. Her daughters stand by the bed, solemn in the slow evening, in the shallows of after supper—Caroline, Nan, and Lucy, her eldest daughter, seventy-two, who holds her hand to help her die, as twenty years past she did the same thing for my father.

Then her breath slows again, as it has done all day. Pink vanishes from cheeks we have kissed so often. and her nostrils quiver. She breathes one more quick breath. Her mouth twitches sharply, as if she speaks a word we cannot hear. Her face is fixed, white, her eyes half-closed. and the next breath never comes.

*   *   *

She lies in a casket covered with gray linen, which my mother and her sisters picked. This is Chadwick's Funeral Parlor in New London, on the ground floor under the I.O.O.F. Her fine hair lies combed on the pillow. Her teeth in her mouth closed, she looks the way she used to, except that her face is tinted, tanned as if she worked in the fields.

This air is so still it has bars. Because I have been thinking about flies, I realize that there are no flies in this room. I imagine a fly wandering in, through these dark-curtained windows, to land on my grandmother's nose.

At the Andover graveyard, Astroturf covers the dirt beside the shaft dug for her. Mr. Jones says a prayer beside the open hole. He preached at the South Danbury Church when my grandmother still played the organ. He raises his narrow voice, that gives itself over to August and blue air, and tells us that Kate in heaven will keep "on growing . . . and growing . . . and growing . . ."—and he stops abruptly, as if the sky had abandoned him, and chose to speak elsewhere through someone else.

*   *   *

After the burial I walk by myself in the barn where I spent summers next to my grandfather. I think of them talking in heaven. Her first word is the word her mouth was making when she died.

In this tie-up a chaff of flies roiled in the leather air, as my grandfather milked his Holsteins morning and night, his bald head pressed sweat-

127

ing into their sides, fat female Harlequins, while their black and white tails swept back and forth, stirring the flies up. His voice spoke pieces he learned for the Lyceum, and I listened crouched on a three-legged stool, as his hands kept time *strp strp* with alternate streams of hot milk, the sound softer as milk foamed to the pail's top.

In the tie-up the spiders feasted like emperors. Each April he broomed the webs out and whitewashed the wood, but spiders and flies came back, generation on generation—like the cattle, mothers and daughters, for a hundred and fifty years, until my grandfather's heart flapped in his chest. One by one the slow Holsteins climbed the ramp into a cattle truck.

✻   ✻   ✻

In the kitchen with its bare hardwood floor, my grandmother stood by the clock's mirror to braid her hair every morning. She looked out the window towards Kearsarge and said, "Mountain's pretty today," or, "Can't see the mountain too good today."

She fought the flies all summer. She shut the screen door *quickly,* but flies gathered on cannisters, on the clockface, on the range when the fire was out, on set-tubs, tables, curtains, chairs. Flies buzzed on cooling lard, when my grandmother made doughnuts. Flies lit on a drip of jam before she could wipe it up. Flies whirled over simmering beans, in the steam of maple syrup. My grandmother fretted, and took good aim with a flyswatter, and hung strips of flypaper behind the range where nobody would tangle her hair in it.

She gave me a penny for every ten I killed. All day with my mesh flyswatter I patrolled kitchen and diningroom, livingroom, even the dead air of the parlor Though I killed every fly in the house by bedtime, when my grandmother washed the hardwood floor, by morning their sons and cousins assembled in the kitchen, like the woodchucks my grandfather shot in the vegetable garden, that doubled and returned, or like the deer that watched for a hundred and fifty years from the brush on Ragged Mountain. and when my grandfather died stalked down the mountainside to graze among peas and corn.

✻   ✻   ✻

We live in their house with our books and pictures, writing poems under Ragged Mountain, gazing each morning at blue Kearsarge.

I dream one night that we live here together, four of us, Jane and I with Kate and Wesley. He milks the cows, she tends sheep and chickens When we wake one morning the two old people are gone, and their animals gone also. In my dream I know they are dead. All morning we look for their bodies in tall grass around barn and chickencoop, until at noon we look up and see them walking the dirt road from West Andover, waving their arms to catch our attention, laughing with pleasure at our surprise, leading a column of giraffes and zebras, ostriches, lions, parrots, gorillas, and tigers up to the house and to the barn.

*   *   *

We live in the house left behind; we sleep in the bed where they whispered together at night. One morning I wake hearing a voice from sleep: "The blow of the axe resides in the acorn."

I get out of bed and drink cold water in the dark morning from the sink's dipper at the window under the sparse oak, and a fly wakes buzzing beside me, cold, and sweeps over set-tubs and range, one of the hundred-thousandth generation.

I planned long ago I would live here, somebody's grandfather.

N. Scott Momaday (1934–   )[47]

THE COLORS OF NIGHT

1. White

An old man's son was killed far away in the Staked Plains. When the old man heard of it he went there and gathered up the bones. Thereafter, wherever the old man ventured, he led a dark hunting horse which bore the bones of his son on its back. And the old man said to whomever he saw:

"You see how it is that now my son consists in his bones, that his bones are polished and so gleam like glass in the light of the sun and moon, that he is very beautiful."

2. Yellow

There was a boy who drowned in the river, near the grove of thirty-two bois d'arc trees. The light of the moon lay like a path on the water, and a glitter of low brilliance shone in it. The boy looked at it and was enchanted. He began to sing a song that he had never heard before; only then, once, did he hear it in his heart, and it was borne like a cloud of down upon his voice. His voice entered into the bright track of the moon, and he followed after it. For a time he made his way along the path of the moon, singing. He paddled with his arms and legs and felt his body rocking down into the swirling water. His vision ran along the path of light and reached across the wide night and took hold of the moon. And across the river, where the path led into the shadows of the bank, a black dog emerged from the river, shivering and shaking the water from its hair. All night it stood in the waves of grass and howled the full moon down.

3. Brown

On the night before a flood, the terrapins move to high ground. How is it that they know? Once there was a boy who took up a terrapin in his hands and looked at it for a long time, as hard as he could look. He succeeded in memorizing the terrapin's face, but he failed to see how it was that the terrapin knew anything at all.

4. Red

There was a man who had got possession of a powerful medicine. And by means of this medicine he made a woman out of sumac leaves and lived with her for a time. Her eyes flashed, and her skin shone like pipestone. But the man abused her, and so his medicine failed. The woman was caught up in a whirlwind and blown apart. Then nothing was left of her but a thousand withered leaves scattered in the plain.

5. Green

A young girl awoke one night and looked out into the moonlit meadow. There appeared to be a tree; but it was only an appearance; there was a shape made of smoke; but it was only an appearance; there was a tree.

6. Blue

One night there appeared a child in the camp. No one had ever seen it before. It was not bad-looking, and it spoke a language that was pleasant to hear, though none could understand it. The wonderful thing was that the child was perfectly unafraid, as if it were at home among its own people. The child got on well enough, but the next morning it was gone, as suddenly as it had appeared. Everyone was troubled. But then it came to be understood that the child never was, and everyone felt better. "After all," said an old man, "how can we believe in the child?" It gave us not one word of sense to hold on to. What we saw, if indeed we saw anything at all, must have been a dog from a neighboring camp, or a bear that wandered down from the high coutry."

7. Purple

There was a man who killed a buffalo bull to no purpose, only he wanted its blood on his hands. It was a great, old, noble beast, and it was a long time blowing its life away. On the edge of the night the people gathered themselves up in their grief and shame. Away in the west they could see the hump and spine of the huge beast which lay dying along the edge of the world. They could see its bright blood run into the sky, where it dried, darkening, and was at last flecked with flakes of light.

8. Black

There was a woman whose hair was long and heavy and black and beautiful. She drew it about her like a shawl and so divided herself from the world that not even Age could find her. Now and then she steals into the men's societies and fits her voice into their holiest songs. And always, just there, is a shadow which the firelight cannot cleave.

Jim Hazard (1936–2012)[48]

THE SNOW CRAZY COPYBOOK 16

Towards sundown the storm broke and I went out for the first time in two days. Snowshoeing in the woods I thought of a poem by Emily Dickinson they had taught us in school. The light, how it was coming across the tips of the pine trees made me think of it.

Well, not the whole poem, just one line was all I called to mind. It was a beaut though, so I "read" that line last night, read it over and over and over. The more I'd read it the more that line would mean.

So after that comes my dream last night. Emily Dickinson and me were (it was one of those dream informations you know without it being said) . . . . Emily and me were married. We were living right here in the shack. Emily is cooking our dinner and I am fixing a snowshoe. My left snowshoe.

She says very casually without looking away from the stove, "You got any plans for this evening, sweetheart?" She just keeps on looking at what she is cooking.

I keep working on the snowshoe. "Now you know," I say very gently, "we just stay here in the shack. We live in the shack all the time, honey."

Emily Dickinson turns to me from the stove. She has been cooking liver and onions (our favorite). I can smell it. I put down the snowshoe. We look at each other real soft. Any peeping tom at the window would see, just that quick, it is True Love between us.

"I was kinda hoping to snowshoe into town," my wife says—not naggy or whiney, just saying the fact—"and maybe sit in the saloon and watch folks play bar dice, you and me have a shot and a beer." Emily Dickinson is so pretty when she's wistful like that she could break your heart.

But I have to say to her: "You *know* I'd like that too but we live in the shack here, Emily." She turns back to the liver and onions, and she's not being sulky or anything. The liver and onions now smell so fine turned brown and golden by Emily Dickinson's small hand. The smell is coming across the room at me, it's coming at me sort of sad and beautiful like afternoon light. It comes to me—and makes me so hungry I am speechless.

"Oh, shoot," Emily Dickinson says, "I know you're right, sweetheart. But you know how it is, just sitting in a saloon with a shot and a beer. Oh come on now, and eat your liver and onions." She dishes it out, still wistful . . . "On a winter afternoon, I do love a saloon . . . you know how it is, hon, it just has that certain slant of—"

I woke up right there. I almost could smell the liver and onions. I had been sleeping on my back. My seeds were still warm in a puddle low on my belly.

Holly Iglesias (1949–   )[49]

NOTHING TO DECLARE

Near the end, there were gold purses and cinch belts and giant sunglasses, men in guayaberas, women with two-carat studs, platinum shrimp forks and rock-crystal ashtrays. I had children then and was free of disease. An undocumented woman ironed in the garage all day long, the same shirts over and over, and a man shocked the pool every other week. They will tell you I left of my own accord, but observe what happens when I smell Paco Rabanne Pour Homme.

* * *

No words precede the reef, none follow. Only sea fans, brain corral, a bank of clouds miles above the surface. The glint of sun, of barracuda and baitfish in flight. The Gulf Stream sweeps by, squeezing between Florida and Cuba, the true Cuba, the solid one, not the wet seduction of dreams. Ahead, the drop, the sea floor sinking, the mask pressing its mark into skin.

* * *

Another afternoon downpour and nothing to do but wait. It will pass, as it passes in Caracas, Havana, San Juan, in all the damp summer places of the hemisphere. Half water, half sugar, Cubans stay inside, they say, so they don't melt. In the battle between Amnesia and Nostalgia, Nostalgia always wins, memories of home solid as sugar or gunmetal, Amnesia a mere vapor wafting through the transom unannounced.

* * *

Bomb, echoic, derives from the Greek for a deep, hollow sound, for when a man eyes the armhole of a sleeveless cotton blouse, gauging what is visible against the sweet ache of all that is potential, assessing with the same easy pleasure his finger takes when circling the headlight of a Lamborghini, and when the tanned arm, the pale breast but inches from the armhole is that of his daughter, thirteen, something detonates, thundering within the body's chambers, seismic at first, then settling into a rumble, its half-life beyond measure.

*   *   *

You depend so on the machete to keep the strangler figs at bay. Forgive me—the plums gone, my letters in the icebox now—I can't sleep, the machete under the bed so cold.

*   *   *

The spoons of people dead before your birth, sterling like this one, the bowl demure, somewhere between demitasse and teaspoon, my great aunt's initials at the bottom, one flourish more ornate than the next. The patina soft, like that of the cream and sugar set my mother bought during the war, which you have, or I suppose you do. I gave it to you when you married, when it looked as though we had made it, as though the knives and lies were behind us. Before the new regime and the hiding of gifts.

*   *   *

Cloudbank flecked peach, ochre, orchid, day dancing with night, the old world with the new. Strains of a distant bolero, the seduction more breeze than gust, a hat with a veil, say, or a lipstick called New Bruise. Body, ocean, melody, all of it fades to a shade neither gray nor blue.

Nin Andrews (1958–)[50]

SNOW MAGIC

The Year Prayer Wasn't Enough

Gil

Whatever you want, you just pray for it, my nanny, Lila May, used to say. But by the year I turned eleven, I knew. Prayer wasn't enough. That year everyone in my school turned mean, and my mama developed a conscience, as she put it, which meant she was always out. If she wasn't at a meeting for the citizens of Gordon County, or delivering cans of Dinty Moore Stew to the local soup kitchen, or going horseback riding with her Hunt Club friends, she was checking on old Mrs. Mellinger, our widow-neighbor who had a habit of getting lost in her own home. *Your mother,* my daddy said, as he poured himself another whiskey, *is always trying to save lost souls.*

Does she ever save them? I asked.

He didn't answer me. He just rattled the ice in his cocktail glass. I could tell by his sad eyes that he missed her as much as I did. My mama and daddy had stopped talking to each other that year, so even when she was home, our house went so quiet it felt like the inside of a funeral parlor before the mourners arrive. On the nights when we sat down to the supper table together, I felt a hush in the air and a chill. As if snow were falling inside each one of us, and no one would make it stop.

Sarah

Confederate Gil

In the town where I grew up, folks were still fighting the Civil War. They blamed the North for all their problems, including taxes, old age, the economy, the rising murder rate, even the tomato wilt and the raspberry blight. My friend, Gil Simmons, bragged that his great-grandpa was wounded in the Battle of Cedar Run. The Simmons lived on the outskirts of town in one of those old plantation homes with white pillars and lace curtains on the windows and acres and acres of green fields with thoroughbreds grazing in them. Gil was an only child, and whenever I visited, he gave me a tour of the bathrooms. All nine of them, not counting the servants' bathrooms. Rumor had it that Mrs. Simmons, or Violet, as my father called her, planned to have an ample family, but Gil was the only child she carried to term. Gil, my daddy said, never looked fully here. He was so pale and thin, he was almost see-through. The town doctor, Dr. Repolt, said Gil was bitten by a spider when he was a bitty thing, and he barely survived. My daddy said Gil looked like he'd been dipped in Clorox. Rumor had it Mr. Simmons wasn't even his daddy. People joked that he was the son of a Confederate soldier, so he was part-ghost. On Halloween Gil's mama dressed him like a ghost in a gray suit with a Confederate flag in one hand, a trick-or-treat bag in the other. *Ghosts aren't gray*, I told him, *and they don't wear uniforms. Yes, they do, too*, he said. *In the South, they do. Casper is a Yankee ghost.*

Gil
Any Place Else

My parents wouldn't let me visit my best friend Sarah Parker's house very often because she lived on the wrong side of town, and I missed her all the time since Sarah and I were what we called twin souls. Which meant we both liked crustless grilled cheese sandwiches cut in triangles (squares never did taste right), and our favorite other things were magic, the numbers 2 and 9, and snow. But we always argued about the color of 9. I said it was blue, but she was sure it was white. How could 9 be white? I'd still like to know. But Sarah said it was simple as a fact, just like pink is a 2. I had to take her word for it because she was the only person I could talk to about things like that. She was the only one who knew the color of numbers and music. How it was scary to feel too good or taste something too sweet like ice cream, which is why I never ate ice cream or Boston cream pies or caramels. I said I didn't care for them, thank you very much. So did Sarah. Back then we even shared lies. But the best part was when she stayed overnight when her folks were out of town, and I couldn't sleep. Neither could she. We snuck into the kitchen and ate bowl after bowl of ice cream. The taste so cold, so sweet, so light.

Hide and Seek

Sarah

My friend Gil's favorite game was hide and seek. We would play it for hours in his huge house that always smelled of Pine-Sol and Old English furniture polish. His house was so big, I never could find him. I was always distracted by the china bowls of chocolates in every room. *Give me a hint,* I'd say, my mouth full of bonbons. Gil would promise to hide in a bathroom next time. But there were so many bathrooms, and some were the size of living rooms. Every one of them had a vanity with a peach-colored marble top and a wooden cabinet full of monogrammed towels. And some of the bathrooms were for the servants. *We don't go in those,* Gil said, his arms on his hips, giving me the stink eye. *But where are the servants?* I asked. I didn't see them. Or hear them. But one day Gil's mama rang a bell for them. And there they were, servants, like a tide rising up from the shadows. *Yes'm, Miz Violet. Yes'm.* Then the servants receded again, vanishing like smoke into the shadows and hallways and basement rooms.

Hair Spray and God's Minions

Gil

My father hated unusual things, and he especially hated my nanny, Lila May, because she was *too damned peculiar. Isn't it strange,* he said, *that a pretty lady like Lila May never married in the first place?* That was the first time I ever looked at her and decided she was pretty, even if she was old. Lila May was the only white woman that ever worked inside our house. Only Mama said she wasn't really white. She was what they called high yeller, but she looked white to me. And she must have been forty years old at least. Her face didn't have any wrinkles or spots, and her waist and ankles were so thin she would have looked girlish if she didn't have a behind the size of two watermelons side by side. Daddy said she had been a beauty contestant once and had been the peach blossom or orange blossom or some kind of blossom queen. He never did ask what kind of blossom she was. He knew she'd say she was God's blossom, and he hated to hear her talk of God and miracles and virgin saints who got the stigmata, and how even their blood smelled like roses and attracted bees in the summertime. The bees always did like Lila May, but I think it was her hairspray that drew them. They'd hover around her, buzzing and buzzing, and she'd say they were all just God's minions. Then she'd glare at me as if to ask, *Who was I to say otherwise?*

Mr. Simmons

Sarah

Gil's daddy, Mr. Simmons, was almost never home when I played at Gil's house. When I asked what his daddy did and where he was, Gil said he was a historian, and that was why he was away. *History,* he explained, *is something you have to search for.* And you have to search not once, but many times. That's what the word, *research,* means. Searching over and over again. His daddy hadn't found it yet, but when he did, he'd be real famous. And everyone would agree at last that the South should have won the War. And the North was to blame. I imagined his daddy coming home with a Confederate soldier in hand who could tell us things we didn't already know. Gil said there were loads of Confederate ghosts around because many of the dead were never buried. He said he could hear them at night. And their ghost dogs, too. Howling for everything they lost. And everything they wanted back again.

Practicing Snow

Gil

The year everything went wrong in my life, Lila May taught me magic. She said all I had to do was sit for a spell. Close my eyes and bring one wish into focus. She said everything else in my mind had to leave. And she meant everything. *It's best to start simple,* she said. *Start with something like the weather. Like a day of sunshine. Or rain.* So I started with snow, even if we did live in the South. I practiced snow at breakfast and at lunch and in the school cafeteria when I was eating my bologna sandwich and Wise Owl potato chips all by myself. I practiced snow after school when Sarah Parker didn't call because she wasn't my friend that day. Sometimes I could touch that snow and taste it. Sometimes I rolled imaginary snow balls and built imaginary snowmen. If I did it right, my toes turned blue, my breath foggy, and a chill ran up my arms and legs. Even my nose ran. Nights I pretended I was falling asleep in snow banks. I kept the windows open, even if the rain gusted in, even if the curtains looked like ghosts flying in the wind. I dreamt I was walking in deep snow, calling out, *Sarah, Sarah!* The snow was falling so thick, like it was answering me with giant white flakes. And I knew, I just knew it would snow soon. One day in early November, it did snow, the heavy flakes falling so fast they covered the ground in a thick, wet blanket. When I told

Lila May that I made that snow, she just smiled. *Of course you did. But don't you tell another soul now. You hear me?*

Snow

Sarah

One snowy day in fifth grade, my friend Gil Simmons bet me five bucks we'd get over a foot of snow. He bet we wouldn't have school the next day. Or the day after that. I bet him we would too have school. But the next day there was so much snow the roof on our tool shed caved in. Two trees toppled over on the power line. I didn't want to get out of bed because we didn't have any heat or electricity, and the house was cold as an ice cube. Mama had to cook over the wood stove, and my daddy couldn't get out of the driveway. Mrs. Mellinger, Gil's crazy old neighbor—we learned later that day—had died in a car wreck. Her tan Ford Falcon slid over to the wrong side of the road, right into oncoming traffic. Two teenagers were in intensive care over at the Martha Jefferson Hospital. My mother said Mrs. Mellinger was drunk and British, and she always did drive on the wrong side of the road, but I blamed Gil. Especially when he phoned all happy, and asked me to pay up. I couldn't believe he would do a thing like that. Neither did my mama. She said she didn't want me playing with Gil Simmons. She said that all the time, but that day I nodded, *Yes ma'am. Gil Simmons isn't even my friend no more.*

Magic

Gil

One day I told Lila May that Sarah Parker was the girl I loved. The next day Sarah Parker gave Timmy Preston, my archenemy, a sweet tart the size of a baseball at recess, so I didn't love her anymore. I told Lila May I didn't care one lick if I ever laid eyes on Sarah Parker again. *Not one lick,* she nodded. *Not one lick.* And when she said it, I knew it was true.

SOURCES

Alexander, Robert. "The American Prose Poem, 1890–1980." PhD diss., University of Wisconsin–Milwaukee, 1982.

———. *White Pine Sucker River*. Minneapolis: New Rivers Press, 1993.

———, ed. *Family Portrait: American Prose Poetry, 1900–1950*. Buffalo: White Pine Press, 2012.

———. ed. *Spring Phantoms: Short Prose by 19th Century British & American Authors*. Buffalo: White Pine Press, 2018.

———. *Finding Token Creek: New and Selected Writing, 1975–2020*. Buffalo: White Pine Press, 2021.

Alexander, Robert, and Dennis Maloney, eds. *The House of Your Dream: An International Collection of Prose Poetry*. Buffalo: White Pine Press, 2008),

Alexander, Robert, Eric Braun, and Debra Marquart, eds. *Nothing to Declare: A Guide to the Flash Sequence*. Buffalo: White Pine Press, 2016.

Alexander, Robert, Mark Vinz, and C. W. Truesdale, eds. *The Party Train: A Collection of North American Prose Poetry*. Minneapolis: New Rivers Press, 1996.

Aristotle. *The Poetics of Aristotle*. Edited and translated by S. H. Butcher. Third Edition Revised. London: Macmillan, 1902.

Bahs, Elizabeth. "On the Threshold: The Polyphonic Poetry Sequence." PhD diss., Royal Holloway, University of London, 2017.

Bakhtin, Mikhail. *Problems of Dostoevsky's Poetics*. Edited and translated by Caryl Emerson. Minneapolis: Univ. of Minnesota Press, 1984.

Bancroft, Corinne. "The Braided Narrative." *Narrative* 26,3 (2018): 262-281. doi:10.1353/nar.2018.0013.

Cohen, Milton A. "Who Commissioned *The Little Review*'s 'In Our Time'?" *Hemingway Review* 23.1 (2003): 106–110.

———. *Hemingway's Laboratory: The Paris in our time*. Tuscaloosa: Univ. of Alabama Press, 2005.

Davenport, Guy. *Introduction to Collected Works,* by Paul Metcalf, 1:i–iv. Minneapolis: Coffee House Press, 1996.

Eisenstein, Sergei. "A Dialectic Approach to Film Form." In *Film Form: Essays in Film Theory,* edited by Jay Leyda, 1–16. New York: Harcourt, Brace, 1949.

Fenollosa, Ernest. "The Chinese Written Character [as a Medium for Poetry]." In *Instigations,* by Ezra Pound, 357–388. New York: Boni and Liveright, 1920.

Fleming, Bruce E. "The Ideogram in Pound and Eisenstein: Sketch for a Theory of Modernism." *Southwest Review* 74.1 (Winter 1989): 87–97.

Hemingway, Ernest. *In Our Time.* Paris: Three Mountains Press, 1924. Reprint: James Gifford, ed. *in our time: The 1924 Text,* by Ernest Hemingway. Victoria, BC: Modernist Versions Project, 2015.

Jolas, Eugene, ed. *transition workshop.* New York: Vagabond, 1949.

Kispert, Peter. "Craft Capsule [#90]: Braided Narratives." In *Poets & Writers,* Online Edition (1 March 2021). https://www.pw.org/content/craft_capsule_braided_narratives.

Lowell, Amy. *Men, Women and Ghosts.* New York: Macmillan, 1916.

Marchesini, Irina. "A new literary genre: Trauma and the individual perspective in Svetlana Aleksievich's *Chernobyl'skaia molitva.*" *Canadian Slavonic Papers* 59 (2017): 313–329.

Meyers, Jeffrey. *Hemingway: A Biography.* New York: Harper & Row, 1985.

Odin, Steve. "The Influence of Traditional Japanese Aesthetics on the Film Theory of Sergei Eisenstein." *Journal of Aesthetic Education* 23.2 (Summer 1989): 69–81.

Perloff, Marjorie. "The Man Who Loved Women: The Medical Fictions of William Carlos Williams." *Georgia Review* 34.4 (Winter 1980): 840–853.

Poe, Edgar Allan. "The Philosophy of Composition." *Graham's Magazine* 28.4 (April 1846): 163–167.

Williams, William Carlos. *Kora in Hell: Improvisations*. Boston: Four Seas, 1920.
———. "For Bill Bird." *Contact* 1.3, N.S. (Oct.1932): 22–34.

Wilson, Edmund. "Mr. Hemingway's Dry Points." *Dial* 77.1 (July 1924): 340–341.

About the Author

Robert Alexander (1949–2023) grew up in Massachusetts. He attended the University of Wisconsin–Madison and for several years taught in the Madison public schools. After receiving his Ph.D. from the University of Wisconsin–Milwaukee, he worked for many years as a freelance editor. From 1993 to 2001, he was a contributing editor at New Rivers Press, serving for the final two years as New Rivers' creative director. Alexander is the founding editor of the Marie Alexander Poetry Series at White Pine Press. He divided his time between southern Wisconsin and the Upper Peninsula of Michigan.

Acknowledgments

White Pine Press has made exhaustive efforts to contact all copyright holders for work included in this book: the authors, their agents, or their heirs. The Press would be grateful for information leading to those we have not been able to find. And to those who have given permission for their work to appear in this anthology, our renewed appreciation.

Grateful acknowledgement to the following authors whose work is reprinted from *Nothing to Declare: A Guide to the Flash Sequence*, ed. Robert Alexander, Eric Braun, and Deb Marquart (Copyright © 2016 by White Pine Press): Nin Andrews, Amy Knox Brown, Carol Guess, Holly Iglesias, Pamela Painter, and Julie Stotz-Ghosh; and to Nina Nyhart for "Ghost Triptych," reprinted from *The House of Your Dream: An International Collection of Prose Poetry*, ed. Robert Alexander and Dennis Maloney (Copyright © 2008 by White Pine Press).

Michael Benedikt: "How to Disembark from a Lark" from *Night Cries* by Michael Benedikt is reprinted by permission of the publisher, Wesleyan University Press. Copyright © 1976 by Michael Benedikt.

Robert Bly: "The Dead Seal" from *The Morning Glory* (Harper & Row, 1975), Copyright © 1975 by Robert Bly, is reprinted by permission of Robert Bly.

Kay Boyle: "January 24, New York," reprinted with the permission of Ian Von Franckenstein.

Emily Holmes Coleman: "The Wren's Nest," reprinted by the permission of Joseph Geraci, executor.

H. D.: "A Prose Chorus" by Hilda Doolittle (H.D.), first published in *Blues: A Magazine of New Rhythms*, copyright © 1929 by Hilda Doolittle, is reprinted by permission of New Directions Publishing Corp., Agent.

Robert Duncan: "Concerning the Maze," copyright 1941, 1968, 2012 by the Jess Collins Trust and used by their permission.

T. S. Eliot : "The Engine" from *Inventions of the March Hare: Poems 1909–1917*

Notes

1-Robert Alexander, "Good Harbor," *White Pine Sucker River* (Minneapolis: New Rivers Press, 1993), 78–81.

2-Robert Alexander, "Maggie May," *Finding Token Creek: New and Selected Writing, 1975–2020* (Buffalo, NY: White Pine Press, 2021), 28.

3-Robert Alexander, "Prose/Poetry," Introduction to *Finding Token Creek*, 17.

4-W. M. Spackman, "Au fil du moi." *Parnassus* 4.1 (Fall–Winter 1975): 189 [189–194]; quoted in Robert Alexander, "Afterword: Supple and Jarring," *Family Portrait: American Prose Poetry, 1900–1950* (Buffalo, NY: White Pine Press, 2012), 231.

5-For the history of in our time, see Milton Cohen, "Who Commissioned The Little Review's 'In Our Time'?" *Hemingway Review* 23.1 (2003) 106–110. See also Jeffrey Meyers, *Hemingway: A Biography* (Da Capo Press, 1999), 141: "Hemingway wrote the first six vignettes of *in our time* in January–February 1923, between the Lausanne Conference and his tour of the Ruhr, and published them in the *Little Review* in the spring of 1923. He completed the remaining twelve sketches in a second concentrated spurt of creativity during late July and early August 1923, between his first trip to Pamplona and his departure for Toronto. He finished nine new stories, which formed the core of *In Our Time*, between January and July 1924, his first six months as a professional writer."

6-Edmund Wilson, "Mr. Hemingeay's Dry Points," *Dial* 77.1 (July 1924): 340–341.

7 Eugene Jolas, ed., *Transition Workshop* (New York: Vagabond, 1949).

8-William Carlos Williams, Prologue to *Kora in Hell: Improvisations* (Boston: Four Seas Co., 1920), 30.

9- Sergei Eisenstein, "A Dialectic Approach to Film Form," in Jay Leyda, ed., *Film Form: Essays in Film Theory* (New York: Harcourt, Brace, 1949), 1–16. Jay Leyda was himself the author of a prose sequence, "It May Have Been the Spring Evening" [etc.], which appeared in *Blues: A Magazine of New Rhythms* 1.8 (Spring 1930), edited by Charles Henri Ford while he was a student at the University of Mississippi. In reference to Eisenstein's discussion of ideograms, it's interesting to consider that Ezra Pound had, nearly a decade earlier, published Ernest Fenollosa's essay, "The Chinese Written Character [as a Medium for Poetry]," in Ezra Pound's *Instigations* (New York: Boni and Liveright, 1920), 357–388. I suspect that Eisenstein was familiar with this work. See: Steve Odin, "The Influence of Traditional Japanese Aesthetics on the Film Theory of Sergei Eisenstein," *Journal of Aesthetic Education* 23.2 (Summer 1989): 69–81; Odin, among other things, discusses how Eisenstein, in 1920, undertook an intensive study of Japanese to facilitate his understanding of the way that the concept of montage was woven into

Japanese culture (p. 75). See also: Bruce E. Fleming, "The Ideogram in Pound and Eisenstein: Sketch for a Theory of Modernism," *Southwest Review* 74.1 (Winter 1989): 87–97.

10-Robert Alexander, "How Does (Prose) Poetry Differ From (Flash) Fiction?" in *Sentence* 8 (2010): 83–84. This piece is excerpted from Alexander, "Afterword: Supple and Jarring," *Family Portrait*—in particular, from "How does the (prose) poem differ from (flash) fiction," 249–255.

11-Jane Heap, "White," in Robert Alexander, ed., *Family Portrait: American Prose Poetry, 1900–1950* (Buffalo, NY: White Pine Press, 2012), 142–143; originally appeared in the *Little Review* 4.7 (Nov. 1917): 5.

12-T. S. Eliot, "The Engine," in Alexander, *Family Portrait*, 117; originally appeared in T. S. Eliot, *Inventions of the March Hare: Poems 1909–1917*, ed. Christopher Ricks (New York: Harcourt, 1996), 90.

13-Thornton Wilder, "Sentences," in Alexander, *Family Portrait*, 209; originally appeared in the Double Dealer 4.21 (Sept. 1922): 110.

14-Robert Bly, "The Dead Seal," in Robert Alexander, Mark Vinz, and C. W. Truesdale, eds., *The Party Train: A Collection of North American Prose Poetry* (Minneapolis: New Rivers Press, 1996), 84–85. Originally appeared in *The Morning Glory* (Harper & Row, 1975), Copyright © 1975 by Robert Bly.

15-Michael Benedikt, "How to Disembark from a Lark," in Robert Alexander, "The American Prose Poem, 1890–1980" (PhD diss., University of Wisconsin–Milwaukee, 1982), 111; originally appeared in Michael Benedikt, *Night Cries* (Middletown, CT: Wesleyan Univ. Press, 1976), 81.

16-Julie Stotz-Ghosh, "Haiku Sequence for Snow," in Robert Alexander, Eric Braun, and Debra Marquart, eds., *Nothing to Declare: A Guide to the Flash Sequence* (Buffalo, NY: White Pine Press, 2016), 248–249.

17-S. H. Butcher, ed. and trans., *The Poetics of Aristotle*, Third Edition Revised (London: Mamillan, 1902), 19.

18-Harrison Garfield Rhodes, "Sketches," in Robert Alexander, ed., *Spring Phantoms: Short Prose by 19th Century British & American Authors* (Buffalo, NY: White Pine Press, 2018), 131–132; originally appeared in the *Chap-Book*, 1.10 (Oct 1, 1894): 259–260. Rhodes was assistant editor of the magazine.

19-H. D., "Prose Chorus," in Alexander, *Family Portrait*, 100–102; originally appeared in *Blues: A Magazine of New Rhythms* 1.5 (June 1929): 105–106.

20-Kay Boyle, "January 24, New York," in Alexander, *Family Portrait*, 77–78; originally appeared in Kay Boyle, Laurence Vail, and Nina Conarain, eds., *365 Days* (New York: Harcourt, 1936), 26.

21-Nina Nyhart, "Ghost Triptych," in Robert Alexander and Dennis Maloney, eds., *The House of Your Dream: An International Collection of Prose Poetry* (Buffalo, NY: White Pine Press, 2008), 134; originally appeared in *The Prose Poem: An International Journal* 2 (1993): Article 56.

22-Pamela Painter, "Art Tells Us . . ." in Alexander, *Nothing to Declare*, 211–216.

23-Mary E. Wilkins [Freeman], "Pastels in Prose," in Alexander, *Spring Phantoms*, 76–81; originally appeared in *Harper's New Monthly Magazine* 86.511 (Dec. 1892), 147–148.

24-Emily Holmes Coleman, "The Wren's Nest," in Alexander, *Family Portrait*, 81–85; originally appeared in *transition 13*, "American Number" (Summer 1928): 215–218.

25-David Young, "Four about Heavy Machinery," in Alexander, "American Prose Poem," 114; originally appeared in David Young, *Work Lights* (Cleveland: Cleveland State Univ. Press, 1977), 16–19.

26-Amy Knox Brown, "Four Episodes in the Life of the Sheridan Boulevard Troll," in Alexander, *Nothing to Declare*, 55–60.

27-Dora Greenwell McChesney, "At Old Italian Casements," in Alexander, *Spring Phantoms*, 133–136; originally appeared in the *Yellow Book* 13 (April 1897): 144–148.

28- Amy Lowell, "Spring Day," *Men, Women and Ghosts* (New York: Macmillan,1916), 330–337; an incomplete version appears in Alexander, *Family Portrait*, 158–162.

29-Robert Duncan, "Concerning the Maze," in Alexander, *Family Portrait*, 112–115; originally appeared in the *Experimental Review*, no. 3 (Sept. 1941): [n.p.].

30--Carol Guess, "Revival of Rosemaling," in Alexander, *Nothing to Declare*, 149–151.

31-Edgar Allan Poe, "The Philosophy of Composition," *Graham's Magazine* 28.4 (April 1846): 163-167.

32-Longer examples include *Five Forks: Waterloo of the Confederacy* and *A Robin's Egg Renaissance: Chicago Modernism & the Great War*.

33-Guy Davenport, Introduction to *Paul Metcalf, Collected Works*, vol I (Minneapolis: Coffee House, 1996), iii, i–ii [i–v].

34- Irina Marchesini, "A new literary genre: Trauma and the individual perspective in Svetlana Aleksievich's Chernobyl'skaia molitva," *Canadian Slavonic Papers* 59 (2017): 313–329.

35-Mikhail Bakhtin, *Problems of Dostoevsky's Poetics*, ed. and trans. Caryl Emerson (Minneapolis: Univ. of Minnesota Press, 1984), 5.

36-Elizabeth Bahs, "On the Threshold: The Polyphonic Poetry Sequence" (PhD diss., Royal Holloway, University of London, 2017), 196, 202.

37-Corinne Bancroft, Abstract, "The Braided Narrative," *Narrative* 26.3 (2018): 262. See, also, Peter Kispert, "Craft Capsule [#90]: Braided Narratives," *Poets & Writers*, Online Edition (1 March 2021); https://www.pw.org/content/craft_capsule_braided_narratives.

38- Robert Alexander, "Library," *Finding Token Creek*, 100–103; originally appeared in Alexander, *White Pine Sucker River*.
Sources for quotes:

1. *The New York Times*, December 11, 1929, quoted by Malcolm Lowry, *Exile's Return: A Literary Odyssey of the 1920s* (1934; rev. ed. New York: Viking Press, 1951), 282.

2. Caresse Crosby, *The Passionate Years* (New York: The Dial Press, 1953), 105.

3. e. e. cummings, as (mis)quoted by Harry Crosby, *Shadows of the Sun: The Diaries of Harry Crosby*, ed. Edward Germain (Santa Barbara: Black Sparrow Press, 1977), 219.

4. Stephen Crosby, letter to his son, quoted by Harry Crosby, *Shadows of the Sun*, 58.

5. Caresse Crosby, *The Passionate Years*, 244.

6. Harry Crosby, "The End of Europe," transition, 16–17 (June, 1929), 119; reprint, *Torchbearer* (Paris: Black Sun Press, 1931), 26.

7. Hart Crane, Postcard to Samuel Loveman, *The Letters of Hart Crane, 1916–1932*, ed. Brom Weber (New York: Hermitage House, 1952), 333.

8. Harry Crosby, *Shadows of the Sun*, 256.

9. Josephine Rotch, telegram to Harry Crosby, quoted by Geoffrey Wolff, *Black Sun: The Brief Transit and Violent Eclipse of Harry Crosby* (New York: Random House, 1976), 209.

10. Archibald MacLeish, quoted by Geoffrey Wolff, *Black Sun*, 312.

11. Harry Crosby, *Shadows of the Sun*, 277.

12. Josephine Rotch Bigelow, telegram to Harry Crosby, quoted by Geoffrey Wolff, *Black Sun*, 285.

13. Harry Crosby, unpublished notebook, quoted by Geoffrey Wolff, *Black Sun*, 283.

14. Josephine Rotch Bigelow, letter to Harry Crosby, quoted by Geoffrey Wolff, *Black Sun*, 285.

15. Archibald MacLeish, quoted by Geoffrey Wolff, *Black Sun*, 288–89.

Much later I wrote another piece about Crosby, "Memoir," which helps contextualize the "sad cautionary tale about the illusion of true love." Followed by "Library," the full piece is titled "The Unknown Harry Crosby: An Homage in Two Voices." It was published in Gian Lombardo, ed., *Seeing with Eyes Closed: The Prose Poems Of Harry Crosby, with Essays by Robert Alexandere and Bob Heman* (Niantic, CT): Quale Press, 2019), 229–236.

39-William Carlos Williams, "For Bill Bird," *Contact* 1.3, N.S. (Oct.1932): 22–34.

40- Marjorie Perloff, "The Man Who Loved Women: The Medical Fictions of William Carlos Williams," *Georgia Review* 34.4 (Winter 1980): 840, 841.

41-Emma Lazarus, "By the Waters of Babylon: Little Poems in Prose," in Alexander, *Spring Phantoms*, 59–63; originally appeared in *The Century*, 33.5 (March 1887): 801–803.

42- Edith Wharton, "The Valley of Childish Things, and Other Emblems," in Alexander, *Spring Phantoms*, 103–108; originally appeared in *The Century* 52.3 (July 1896): 467–469; reprinted in *The Collected Short Stories of Edith Wharton*, ed. R. W. B. Lewis, 2 vols. (New York: Scribner, 1968), 1:58–63.

43-Fenton Johnson, "African Nights," in Alexander, *Family Portrait*, 152–157; originally appeared in Alfred Kreymborg, ed., *Others for 1919: An Anthology of the New Verse* (New York: Nicholas L. Brown, 1920), 77–82.

44- Ernest Hemingway, *In Our Time* (Paris: Three Mountains Press, 1924); an incomplete version appears in Alexander, *Family Portrait*. The following note appeared at the end of the Three Montains edition: "Here ends The Inquest into the state of contemporary English prose, as edited by Ezra Pound and printed at the Three Mountains Press." This rare book has finally been reprinted: James Gifford, ed., *in our time: The 1924 Text*, by Ernest Hemingway (BC: Modernist Versions Project, 2015).

45- Kay Boyle, "Summer," in Alexander, *Family Portrait*, 71–74; originally appeared in *This Quarter* 1.1 (Spring 1925): 40–42.

46- Donald Hall, "Flies," in Alexander, *Party Train*, 159–162; originally appeared in Donald Hall, *Kicking the Leaves* (New York: Harper & Row, 1978), 38–42.

47- N. Scott Momaday, "The Colors of Night," in Alexander, "American Prose Poem," 96–97; originally appeared in N. Scott Momaday, *The Gourd Dancer* (New York: Harper & Row, 1976), 44–46.

48-Jim Hazard, "The Snow Crazy Copybook 16," in Alexander, *Party Train*, 173–174; originally appeared in *Minnesota Review* 6 (Spring 1976), 19–20, and was collected in the longer sequence, "The Snow Crazy Copybook," in James Hazard, *Hive of Souls: Selected Poems, 1968–1976* (Trumansburg, NY: Crossing Press, 1977).

49-Holly Iglesias, "Nothing to Declare," in Alexander, *Nothing to Declare*, 168–170.

50-Nin Andrews, "Snow Magic," in Alexander, *Nothing to Declare*, 25–31.